SQL Server Without All the Nonsense

Gregory Gavarian
2021

Acknowledgements

I would like to extend my thanks to those who have helped me get to where I am today, as well as those who have proofread this book. To my friend Justin Ziske, who, on a brisk weekend back in February of 2015, first explained to me what SQL is after describing his job to me, to which I followed up by asking, "Oh yeah, I've heard of that before, what exactly is it?" To my former supervisor Rob Louie, who took a chance with me and gave me my first position in the field of analytics, and whom I incessantly bugged for help with queries while I learned on the job. To Diego Oliveros, who did the majority of the proofreading for this book and inspired me to move on to bigger and better opportunities. To Uncle Tom, who also proofread some of the early drafts of this book. And to Krikor Ghazarian, who had no hand in the shaping of my career or the making of this book, but is an awesome friend, anyway.

Dedication

To my friends at home, my friends at work, and my family.
But most importantly, to Alicia; my girlfriend when I started this
book, my fiancée by the time I published it, and perhaps,
by the time you read this, my wife.

Table of Contents

11 Appendix A: Indexes 157

12 Appendix B: Selected Functions 167

13 Index 213

14 Glossary 221

1 Introduction

1.1 Who Is This Book For?

This book is intended for those who need to learn, but don't have much time to dedicate to doing it. You're busy in the morning, and busy during work. You come home from work, you need to run errands, cook dinner, clean up, shower, and prep for tomorrow. By the time you're finished, it's 10 o'clock at night and you simply want to relax.

This is the book for those who need to fit learning into the gaps in their day. A little bit before bed, the half an hour you have during lunch at your desk, or the 45-minute commute on the train. We're all busy people. Sometimes we don't have the luxury of carving out a chunk of the day to sit down and thoroughly immerse ourselves in a programming book.

You can say that this book is the book I *wish* I had when I started learning SQL. When scouring the web for introductory books to learn a specific language, I come across far too many that are filled with information that is above the level of a novice user. Another common thing I see is having lengthy chapters on setting up your system just to be *able* to start: *install this program, and then install this other program, download the code from this repository, extract these files to a new directory in the root of your C: drive, set up these system variables, etc.* You'd better hope that none of those instructions are outdated and that everything goes smoothly, or your quest to learn more has paused before it's even begun. What's more, the author typically introduces third-party applications that are *his* personal preference, and writes the entire book according to it.

Other things I run into quite often are books that heap on so much theory that they account for a significant chunk of the book. One example in particular was a 275-page book, that got to the actual programming lessons on page *100*. Almost 40% of that book is *not* teaching you the language. That's not to say that theory is not important, but sitting through hours of a music theory class doesn't teach you how to play a guitar. There's no replacement for hands-on practice.

I am primarily aiming this book towards people who work in an analytical field, who may use Microsoft Excel to do some work, but need to scale up due to the amount of data they need to churn through. Any company that handles large volumes of data will probably use SQL in some way. Analysts are typically given some space on the computer servers that they can play around in to freely develop and test SQL code in, without the risk of messing up actual important data. This is usually referred to as the "development environment," or the "sandbox." The best approach to utilizing this book will be to copy some of the real data over into your sandbox space, and work with that (we'll learn how to create and copy data in the coming chapters).

With a title like *SQL Server Without All the Nonsense*, you should expect a tighter focus on practical skills, with less of an emphasis on theory. There are no exercises for you to complete; your exercises will be leveraging these chapters with the data your company has available. Being able to practice on actual data from your company will be the quickest approach to becoming a trusted resource for SQL work. If, for some reason, you cannot do this at the office, and must do it on your home computer, the following chapters have information on installing and setting up the necessary programs. Websites like https://www.kaggle.com have free data sets for you to download and practice with.

There will be times when I claim that something cannot be done in a certain fashion, when in reality, it is possible. However, to go into all of the nuances and minor details in depth would make the book needlessly complex and likely confuse the reader. Therefore, I have chosen to omit these as they will detract from the important lessons in each chapter. Similarly, when describing certain functions or functionality of SQL, I will only cover the most common scenarios. It would be impossible to describe every possible use case while keeping the book succinct.

1.2 What is SQL?

SQL, or the **S**tructured **Q**uery **L**anguage, is used to interact with (or "speak to") a database, a collection of data objects like tables, which store information. By executing commands in SQL, known as "queries," users may ask the database to retrieve and display stored data from these tables, create objects, insert new data, or alter existing data. This data can be anything, information about people, accounts on a website, purchases, historical events, etc. Typically, SQL is used by members of a business intelligence or data analyst team.

SQL was created in the 1970's by Raymond Boyce and Donald Chamberlin, and was originally named SEQUEL, which stood for **S**tructured **E**nglish **Que**ry **L**anguage. SEQUEL was used to interact with data on IBM's database management system, System R.

The name SEQUEL was later changed to SQL due to a trademark infringement. In 1986, SQL became a standard of the American National Standards Institute (ANSI) for interacting with a database. One year later, it became a standard of the International Organization for Standardization (ISO).

Since its introduction, SQL has undergone several major revisions, each of which added new functionality. These enhancements allow the user to perform more complex tasks with less code, and less of an impact on the system. The more you learn about these functions, the more your queries will become thorough, elegant, and efficient, hallmarks of a good analyst.

1.3   What is SQL Server?

SQL Server is Microsoft's implementation of a database management system (DBMS). Users can interact with the data contained in the DBMS by sending queries to the server or computer running SQL Server. More often than not, these queries interact with tables containing data.

There are many different DBMSs. Aside from SQL Server, some popular ones are:

- Oracle Database by Oracle Corporation
- PostgreSQL by the PostgreSQL Global Development Group
- Db2 by IBM
- Teradata by Teradata Corporation

While the syntax across all platforms is generally the same, each system utilizes a slightly different form of the SQL language. The language used with SQL Server is known as Transact-SQL or T-SQL. From here on, when I refer to the SQL language, I'm actually referring to the T-SQL language. Some of the syntax used in the T-SQL language will *only* work with SQL Server, and may not be compatible with other management systems. The same is true for the examples within this book; they will work with SQL Server, but may not work with other systems. Additionally, this book was written with SQL Server 2019 in mind. Some features and functions may not be available in earlier versions. If a new version of SQL Server has been released by the time you read this, don't worry. The language doesn't change *that* much from version to version.

1.4 SQL Server Management Studio (SSMS)

SQL Server Management Studio (SSMS) is a software application that is used to administer different parts of SQL Server, as well as interact with data. It allows users to view and create different databases and tables, as well as send SQL queries to SQL Server which can modify data or return data to the user.

Unlike the T-SQL language, SSMS is *not* required to interact with SQL Server. It serves a convenient graphical interface which organizes many common commands into buttons and menu items for easy access. Several third-party applications exist which are able to interact with multiple DBMSs in one unified platform, rather than one proprietary application for each DBMS. One such application popular with businesses is TOAD Data Point by Quest Software.

For the purposes of this book, you will be using SSMS to create and execute queries. However, since SSMS is not explicitly required to execute SQL queries, nor is this a guidebook on the software, I will be keeping information on SSMS to a minimum. While tasks such as creating a table can be accomplished by selecting items within the menus of SSMS, I will not cover these, and will instead focus on the queries used to accomplish them, because these commands are often transferrable to other DBMSs (albeit with a little bit of tweaking).

1.5   Installing SQL Server and SSMS

Go to https://www.microsoft.com/en-us/sql-server/sql-server-downloads and look for a download link to SQL Server Express. At the time of writing, the current version of SQL Server is 2019. Click the download link for the installation file and open it when it is complete. Choose "Basic" when prompted.

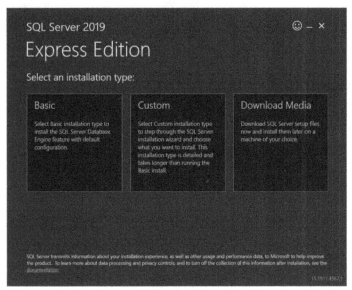

Figure 1-1

Follow through the prompts until it finishes installing, and eventually you'll reach the following screen.

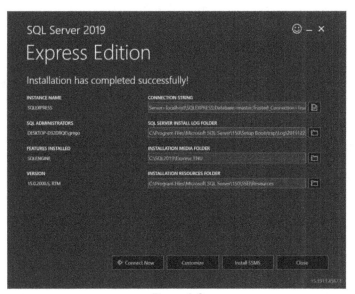

Figure 1-2

On this screen, click "Connect Now." A command prompt will appear confirming that you can connect to the new installation of SQL Server. Next, click Install SSMS, or go to https://docs.microsoft.com/en-us/sql/ssms/download-sql-server-management-studio-ssms and look for the download link for SSMS. At the time of writing, the current version of SSMS is 18.4. Follow through the prompts until it finishes installing, and close the installation window.

1.6   Navigating and Using SSMS

After installing SSMS, open it by double clicking on the icon (Figure 1-3) that was created on your desktop, or by searching for it in the Windows start menu.

Figure 1-3

The splash screen for SSMS will pop up, followed by the main program. You will be greeted with a screen similar to the following figure.

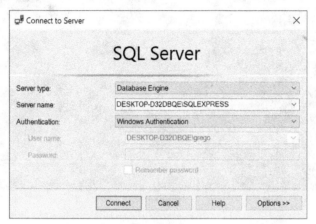

Figure 1-4

The server name should automatically be populated as well as the "User name" field if you are using the Windows Authentication. If the server name is not populated, it is the name of your computer, followed by a backslash and *SQLEXPRESS*. Now you may click "Connect," and you will be greeted with the full SSMS.

On the left side of the screen, you will see a box called the "Object Explorer." This is where you will browse through different databases, and be able to see all tables and related information. You can dive deeper into each folder and database by clicking the + box next to it. Later, when you create tables and databases, if you don't see them immediately reflected in the object explorer, try right-clicking on the parent folder and clicking "Refresh."

Figure 1-5

Eventually, when we create our first database, we will use a query to do so. At the top left, under the main toolbar, there is a button labeled "New Query." If you cannot find the button, you may use the keyboard shortcut Ctrl+N. When you click it, a new window will appear where you can create and edit queries.

A query can be run by clicking the "Execute" button, or by pressing F5. When a query is run, a new window will appear at the bottom of the editor displaying the results of the query and/or messages. When you are finished writing a query, you can save your query by pressing Ctrl+S, or by going through the File menu.

1.7 Conventions used in this book

This book uses several conventions to differentiate between queries, query results, syntaxes, tables, etc.

Code blocks are utilized heavily. Any SQL code that is broken out from the rest of the text will be surrounded by a border, and will be either a SQL syntax (to give a rough idea of how a statement is composed) or a full SQL query. Occasionally, a code block will represent the *incorrect* way to write a query. This code will be surrounded by a dashed line.

Syntaxes will have the caption Syntax #-#. The following code is an example of what a syntax may look like. This particular syntax appears in the next chapter.

```
SELECT Columns
  FROM Table
```
Syntax 1-1

In syntaxes, anything that is written in both ***bold and italics*** is a field that must be supplied by the user. In Syntax 1-1, SELECT and FROM do not need to be changed, but ***columns*** and ***table*** must be changed to reflect the names of actual columns, from an actual table (the concept of columns and tables will be introduced shortly).

Queries will have the caption Query #-# and will utilize the syntaxes in the context of the current chapter. Query 1-1 shows how the earlier syntax would be changed to reflect a real table and the columns within it.

```
SELECT CustomerName,
       StreetAddress,
       PurchaseDate,
       PurchasePrice,
       PaymentMethod
  FROM dbo.CustomerPurchaseInfo
```
Query 1-1

The formatting of the code does not affect the query or the results. The formatting of Query 1-1 is a personal preference. It could have been written as shown in Query 1-2 and the results would have been the same.

```
SELECT CustomerName, StreetAddress, PurchaseDate, PurchasePrice, PaymentMethod FROM
dbo.CustomerPurchaseInfo
```
Query 1-2

SQL queries are supposed to end with a semicolon, but this is generally unnecessary. Most queries will execute without one. There are a few scenarios in which it is necessary to end a query with a semicolon, and any scenarios that require it will be outlined in the text when the situation arises.

Outside of code blocks, the conventions are different. Tables are referred to in *italics*, and columns are referred to in **bold**. For example, "This query will select **CustomerName** and **StreetAddress** from the table *dbo.CustomerPurchaseInfo*."

When actually showing the data within a table, the text will show a grid with the name of the table on the top in italics, and each column within the table will be shown with a bold heading, with the data underneath. Each table will also show the caption Table #-# underneath.

For example:

dbo.SampleTable	
SampleName	**SampleBirthday**
Theresa Nickerson	1978-08-16
Barbara Suggs	1984-08-03
Hector Parsons	1994-12-08
Cecil Mason	1982-02-07

Table 1-1

When showing the results of a query, they will appear similar to Table 1-1 except the heading of the entire table will be "Query Results."

2 Creating and Modifying Databases and Tables

A database is a collection of data, structured into discrete objects known as "tables." These tables can be thought of as a grid of rows and columns. Each row, or record, may contain the details of an event, or a customer's account, or any data deemed necessary to save for later use, while each column represents a single attribute about the row. If the table contains the information for customers of an online retailer, each row will represent one customer, while each *column* describes something about the customer, such as their name, account number, street address, city, zip code, email address, etc.

2.1 Creating and Deleting Databases

Before any tables can be created, a database must be created. A database can be created in a single query, the syntax for which is shown below.

```
CREATE DATABASE Database Name
```
Syntax 2-1

After executing a query similar to Syntax 2-1, a database with the supplied name will be created, and tables can be created within it. To see the database reflected in the object explorer (Figure 1-5), right click on the parent database folder and click "Refresh." You are allowed to have more than one database at a time, and one query can access tables across multiple databases.

A database can be deleted by replacing CREATE in Syntax 2-1 with DROP.

```
DROP DATABASE Database Name
```
Syntax 2-2

2.2 Data types

Likely any table you work with will have multiple columns comprising different types of data. One column might store dates, one might store numbers, and others might store words, phrases, or other alphanumeric information (strings). As such, SQL requires each column to have a dedicated data type.

The following tables list common data types that are widely used in real-world applications of SQL. The "invoking within code" column will be utilized later in chapter 2.3.

Data Type	Values Allowed	Invoking Within Code
Bit	0 or 1	`Bit`
Tiny Integer	Integers from 0 to 255	`TinyInt`
Small Integer	Integers from -2^{15} to $2^{15}-1$	`SmallInt`
Integer	Integers from -2^{31} to $2^{31}-1$	`Int`
Big Integer	Integers from -2^{63} to $2^{63}-1$	`BigInt`
• Decimal • Numeric	• Any number from $-10^{38}+1$ to $10^{38}-1$ • Total number of digits (left and right of the decimal point) cannot exceed 38. The total number of digits is referred to as the "precision," p. • Number of digits to the right of the decimal point cannot exceed the number of digits to the left of the decimal point. The number of digits to the right are referred to as the "scale," s.	• `Decimal(`p`, `s`)` • `Numeric(`p`, `s`)` (Both styles can be used interchangeably.)

Table 2-1

Data Type	Values Allowed	Invoking Within Code
Date	Jan. 1st, 0001 through Dec. 31st, 9999	`Date`
Date and time	Date: Jan. 1st, 1753 through Dec. 31st, 9999 Time: 00:00:00 through 23:59:59.997	`Datetime`

Table 2-2

Character Strings	Values Allowed	Invoking Within Code
Character	• Characters must belong to the Unicode character set. • Number of characters must not exceed the declared length, n. • String values shorter than the declared length will be padded with spaces to fill in the remaining space.	`Char(`n`)`
Variable-Length Character	• Characters must belong to the Unicode character set. • Number of characters must not exceed the declared length, n, or 2 GB if **max** is chosen as the length.	• `Varchar(`n`)` • `Varchar(max)`

Table 2-3

To differentiate strings and dates from numerical expressions when writing a query, the entire expression must be surrounded with apostrophes, meaning that 5 is interpreted as a number, while '5' is interpreted as a string. Similarly, 2020-06-03 is interpreted as a mathematical expression (2,020-6-3 = 2,011), while '2020-06-03' means June 3rd, 2020.

Dates in this book are written in *YYYY-MM-DD* form. This style conforms to ISO 8601, which is meant to define an unambiguous way of writing dates. Someone living in the United States would probably say that 5/4/2020 is May 4th, 2020, while someone living in Europe would probably say the 5th of April, 2020. In *YYYY-MM-DD* form, there is no question as to which date is being referred to. While SQL will handle dates in *MM/DD/YYYY* form, the safest choice it to use *YYYY-MM-DD* form.

2.3 Creating Tables

Before moving any further, I mentioned earlier that queries can span multiple databases. With this in mind, how can we ensure that when a query is executed, that it is pointing to the correct database? We'll soon learn the proper query to execute to create a table, but unless that table is created where we want it, it's kind of pointless. There are two common methods to solve this issue. The first method is to qualify every table name with the database that it is contained within. If a table named *dbo.SampleTable* is contained within a database named *SampleDatabase*, the fully qualified table would be *SampleDatabase.dbo.SampleTable*. The second method is to specify in the beginning of the query which database to use. This is accomplished with USE.

```
USE Database Name
```
Syntax 2-3

If USE is invoked at the start of a query, any of the proceeding tables that reside within that database do *not* need to be fully qualified. Only tables outside of that database need to be qualified. Going forward, it will be assumed that all tables and objects are in the same (and only) database, meaning that the USE command will not be shown, nor will table names be fully qualified. This is purely a stylistic choice to make sample code snippets shorter. Now, back to the lesson.

When creating a new table from scratch, the query must start with CREATE TABLE.

```
CREATE TABLE Table Name
(
    1st Column Name    Data Type    Allow NULL,
    2nd Column Name    Data Type    Allow NULL,
    ...
    Nth Column Name    Data Type    Allow NULL
)
ON [PRIMARY]
```
Syntax 2-4

There is a minimum of four fields that must be entered. The first is the desired name of the table. Next is what the name of the first column will be. But be careful, certain words may be among those that SQL reserves for internal use. It is best to avoid using such names (such as naming a column "date," since you risk conflating the name of the column and the data type), but if it is necessary, the use of reserved words can be achieved by enclosing the name in square brackets, [and].

The remaining two fields are the type of data that the column will contain, and whether or not null values will be allowed. A null represents a value that is missing, unknown, or does not exist. If a column should allow null values, *allow NULL* should be replaced with NULL, otherwise, it should be replaced with NOT NULL. If there will be multiple columns in the table, you may place a comma after *allow NULL* and continue on to defining the next column.

A query that creates a table will generally end with the phrase ON [PRIMARY]. You need not worry about what this means, as it is above the level of this book. If you have all of this information filled out, you can execute the query, and the table will be created.

As a demonstration, I'll create a table named *dbo.PersonInformation* with three columns. The first column, **PersonName**, will be a variable-length string of 20 characters, and null values will not be allowed. The second column, **Age**, will be an integer and *will* allow null values. The final column, **BirthDate**, will be a date, and will also allow null values.

The *data type* field will utilize the "invoking within code" columns from chapter 2.2. For **PersonName**, the data type will be varchar(20), for **Age** it will be int, and for **BirthDate** it will be date. You've likely noticed that every table I've referred to has the prefix *dbo* in front of it. This is referred to as the *schema*, and should not be adjusted.

```
CREATE TABLE dbo.PersonInformation
(
      PersonName varchar(20) NOT NULL,
      Age int NULL,
      BirthDate date NULL
) ON [PRIMARY]
```

Query 2-1

The table *dbo.PersonInformation* will be created when this query is executed. But until rows are added, this table will be empty. To see the table reflected in the object explorer (Figure 1-5), navigate to your database and click the + box on the left to expand it. In the folder list that appears, right click on the "Tables" folder, and click "Refresh." At this point, even if you disconnect from SQL Server, the table will not disappear.

2.4   Inserting Data

2.4.1   Manually Inserting New Data

The INSERT command is used to add rows to a table. The values that will appear in each column are supplied by the user in the query.

```
INSERT INTO Target Table
     VALUES (1st Value, 2nd Value, … Nth Value)
```
Syntax 2-5

There is a minimum of two fields that must be entered. The first is the name of the table that the rows will be inserted into. The second is a list of the individual values that will compose a single row. A single row begins with a parenthesis, followed by the individual values, separated by commas, and lastly, a closing parenthesis. In this format, the first value inside the parentheses will be placed into the first column of the table, the second value into the second column, etc.

If multiple rows will be inserted via a single query, you can place a comma after the closing parenthesis of the previous row, and repeat the process of placing a parenthesis, listing the values, etc. Up to 1,000 rows at a time can be inserted using this method.

Let's actually insert some rows into the table that was created before, *dbo.PersonInformation*. Since the table contains three columns, three values will be necessary to insert a row, the person's name, age, and birth date. For simplicity's sake, the person's name will be "John Doe," born on January 1st, 1980, which would make him 41 years old at the time of writing.

```
INSERT INTO dbo.PersonInformation
     VALUES ('John Doe', 41, '1980-01-01')
```
Query 2-2

dbo.PersonInformation		
PersonName	Age	BirthDate
John Doe	41	1980-01-01

Table 2-4

The same process can be followed for inserting multiple rows.

```
INSERT INTO dbo.PersonInformation
     VALUES ('Jane Doe', 23, '1998-02-01'),
            ('John Q Public', 28, '1993-03-01')
```
Query 2-3

dbo.PersonInformation		
PersonName	Age	BirthDate
John Doe	41	1980-01-01
Jane Doe	23	1998-02-01
John Q Public	28	1993-03-01

Table 2-5

2.4.2   Importing Data from a File

Realistically speaking, you'll probably never insert data into a table row-by-row. Instead, you will likely have a file that you need to load into a new or pre-existing table. For example, you wish to upload the file below into a new table. This is a comma-separated values file, with the extension *.CSV*. The first row in the file represents the column names, and each successive row represents a single row of data. In each row, there are three values, separated from each other by commas[1].

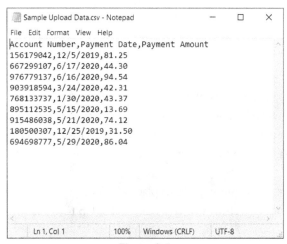

Figure 2-1

To import data from a file, right click on the database you want to import into, hover over "Tasks," and then click "Import Data." The following screen will pop up.

Figure 2-2

Click Next, and in the dropdown box, select "Flat File Source." Click the browse button, and select the file that you wish to upload. You may have to adjust the dropdown box above the "Open" button to show CSV files as well. The import window should now look something like the following figure.

---

[1] There are many different types of files, delimited text files, fixed-width text files, Excel files, etc. Care must be taken if the values inside the row contain the delimiter. E.g., what if you had a comma separated file, and one of the values was **Smith, John**? Is the comma supposed to be a delimiter, or is it supposed to be included as part of the value? There are too many cases to cover individually, so I will only be focusing on the simplest and most common case, a comma-separated file that does *not* run into this potential issue.

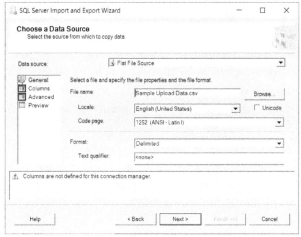

Figure 2-3

Click Advanced on the left side, and you'll see each column name which was parsed out from the first row in the CSV file. You'll notice that on the right side, the *DataType* field has a dropdown box which allows you to select the type and size of the data contained within that column. In the screenshot below, **Account Number** is currently set up as a string with a length of 50. Since none of the account numbers exceed nine digits, this should be sufficient.

The import wizard will attempt to select the best data type, but it doesn't always work well. **Payment Date** was brought in as a string as well, but you can pick either DT_DATE or DT_DBDATE from *DataType*. Lastly, **Payment Amount** can be set up as a NUMERIC, at which point you can define what the scale and precision is. Additionally, in the *Name* field, you can adjust what the name of the column will be in the table that is created (typically spaces are removed).

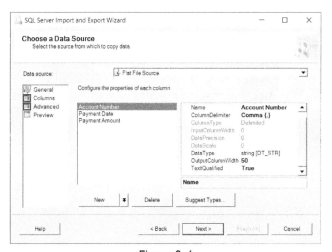

Figure 2-4

Click Next, expand the Destination dropdown box, scroll all the way to the bottom, and select "SQL Server Native Client ##.#." Click Next again, and you'll have the option to name the table. The default name is the name of the file, but you can change it here (remember, don't adjust the *dbo*). If the name you enter is the name of a table that is already in the database, the import wizard will attempt to append your file into the table, otherwise it will become its own new table. Finally, click Next, Finish, and then Finish again, the import wizard will then import your file, and your new table will be created (or the file will be appended to the table).

2.5 Precautions When Inserting Rows

There are some important caveats to know when attempting to insert a row.

First, the values to be inserted must obey the definitions of the columns that they are being inserted into. Attempting to insert a null value into a column that does not allow them will result in an error and a failed insert. The same applies to overflowing a column (though there are some exceptions, seen in chapter 2.6). Attempting to insert a string that is fifteen characters long into a column that is only set up for ten characters will also result in an error and a failed insert.

The next is that (in most cases) the number of values listed inside the parenthesis *must* be equal to the number of columns in the target table. If a table contains five columns, and only four values are listed, SQL may not know how to handle the missing value, and the insert will fail. This is also true if SQL attempts to insert six values into a table which contains five columns. Columns can be created such that if no value is provided during an insertion, they will assume a default value, but that will not be covered.

The last is that unless special precaution is taken, the order of the values inside the parentheses must match the order of the columns in the target table. If Query 2-2 had the positions of John Doe and 41 reversed, SQL would attempt to insert 41 as a string into **PersonName**, and John Doe as an integer into **Age**[2]. This would not work, and the insert would fail.

The only way to list values in a different order than the columns in the target table is to inform SQL that they will be appearing in a different order. This is done by placing a parenthesis after the table name, and listing the columns in the same order that the values appear in. Query 2-4 shows how Query 2-2 would appear if we were to accommodate for the reversal of the values intended for **PersonName** and **Age**.

```
INSERT INTO dbo.PersonInformation (Age, PersonName, BirthDate)
     VALUES (41, 'John Doe', '1980-01-01')
```
Query 2-4

With this method, the first value in the list, 41, does *not* accidentally get inserted into **PersonName**. SQL was informed that the first value in the list will go into **Age**, and that the second value will go into **PersonName**.

---

[2] SQL can perform what's known as an *implicit* conversion. Even though 41 is not a string, it can be converted to a string and then inserted into the table successfully (the conversion is handed entirely by SQL). The problem arises when it attempts to convert John Doe to a number. This is impossible, which causes the insert to fail.

2.6 Altering Tables and Columns

It is possible to adjust a table after creating it. This is done with the ALTER command.

```
ALTER TABLE Table Name
Perform Action
```
Syntax 2-6

After invoking ALTER, SQL must be given instructions on what exactly to do with the table. The most common thing to do is to add or drop a column. These are done with the ADD and DROP COLUMN commands. When adding a column to a table, you do not need to write COLUMN after ADD. The syntax for adding a column must include the column definition, similar to Syntax 2-4.

```
ALTER TABLE Table Name
        ADD New Column Name    Data Type    Allow NULL
```
Syntax 2-7

Suppose that we needed to add an additional column, **HairColor**, a variable-length string of ten characters with nulls allowed, to *dbo.PersonInformation*.

```
ALTER TABLE dbo.PersonInformation
        ADD HairColor varchar(10) NULL
```
Query 2-5

dbo.PersonInformation			
PersonName	Age	BirthDate	HairColor
John Doe	41	1980-01-01	NULL
Jane Doe	23	1998-02-01	NULL
John Q Public	28	1993-03-01	NULL

Table 2-6

The column **HairColor** has been added to the table. When adding a new column to a pre-existing table, all of the values in that column will be null. The opposite operation to adding a column would be *removing* a column.

```
ALTER TABLE Table Name
DROP COLUMN Column Name
```
Syntax 2-8

Suppose now that we decided we didn't need to add **HairColor**, and we wish to remove it.

```
ALTER TABLE dbo.PersonInformation
DROP COLUMN HairColor
```
Query 2-6

After executing this query, *dbo.PersonInformation* will revert to how it originally was in Table 2-5.

Another option for altering a table is to change the definition of a column. The syntax for altering a column must include the name of the table, the name of the column, and the new definition of the column.

```
ALTER TABLE Table Name
ALTER COLUMN Column Name    New Data Type
```

Syntax 2-9

The following table, *dbo.AlterColumnTest*, has been created with one column that is a decimal data type with a precision of ten, and a scale of two (ten total digits, two of which are to the right of the decimal point).

dbo.AlterColumnTest
DecimalValue
15.14
19.17
254.09
45.83

Table 2-7

What will happen if we attempt to insert the value 90.107 into the table? Contrary to what you may think, SQL does not throw an error.

dbo.AlterColumnTest
DecimalValue
15.14
19.17
254.09
45.83
90.11

Table 2-8

SQL instead *rounds* the decimal value to the scale as defined by the column. If we needed three decimal places, we could execute Query 2-7. After executing it, all values will be written out to three decimal places.

```
ALTER TABLE dbo.AlterColumnTest
ALTER COLUMN DecimalValue decimal(10,3)
```

Query 2-7

dbo.AlterColumnTest
DecimalValue
15.140
19.170
254.090
45.830
90.110

Table 2-9

Now if we insert the value 90.107, the number will be accurately reflected in the table.

dbo.AlterColumnTest
DecimalValue
15.140
19.170
254.090
45.830
90.110
90.107

Table 2-10

What about a scenario in which we change the data type to something that is *less* precise, such as going from a decimal to an integer? In this case, the values will be rounded towards zero (not to the nearest integer). E.g., 10.95 will be rounded down to 10. And similarly, -10.95 will be rounded up to -10.

There are more advanced commands you can use in conjunction with the ALTER TABLE command, but they will not be covered here.

2.7 Dropping Tables

When a table is no longer needed, it can be deleted from the database[3]. This is done using the DROP command, similar to when deleting an entire database.

```
DROP TABLE Table Name
```
Syntax 2-10

When a table is dropped, it is removed entirely from the database. This is different from clearing the contents of a table (described later in chapter 9.2). If *dbo.PersonInformation* was no longer needed, the following query would delete it.

```
DROP TABLE dbo.PersonInformation
```
Query 2-8

If one attempts to query against the table after dropping it, SQL will return an error message stating that *dbo.PersonInformation* is an invalid object.

---

[3] Only drop a table if you are *absolutely sure* that it is no longer needed. In an office environment, many important reports may rely on a single table. If you accidentally drop one of these tables, expect some very angry emails to be headed your way.

3 Choosing and Filtering Columns

3.1 Selecting Columns

Chapter 2 focused on how to create, alter, and delete tables, and also how to insert data into them, but not how to retrieve data *from* them. Nearly all queries that retrieve data will use SELECT.

```
SELECT Columns
  FROM Table
```

Syntax 3-1

Two fields are required to return data from a table, a list of the desired columns, separated by commas, and the name of the table that the columns reside in (a FROM clause and a table are not always required, but that will be covered later). As a sample, I have created a table of purchases, *dbo.CustomerPurchaseInfo*, at a fictional clothing company and inserted some data into it. There are five columns, **CustomerName**, **StreetAddress**, **PurchaseDate**, **PurchasePrice**, and **PaymentMethod**.

```
SELECT CustomerName,
       StreetAddress,
       PurchaseDate,
       PurchasePrice,
       PaymentMethod
  FROM dbo.CustomerPurchaseInfo
```

Query 3-1

CustomerName	StreetAddress	PurchaseDate	PurchasePrice	PaymentMethod
Gail Curran	3920 Arthur Rd	2020-04-12	53.4	Credit card
Peter Gray	2054 College Vw	2020-04-13	106.23	Credit card
Nicholas Hill	4427 Losh Ave	2020-04-17	82.11	Cash
Julie Moss	4506 Oliver Ave	2020-04-19	30.33	Cash
Lela Girard	3554 Stuart St	2020-04-23	87.93	Credit card

Query Results

Table 3-1

The order of the columns in a SELECT query does not have to match the order of the columns in the table. Query 3-2 is perfectly valid and will generate the same result set as Query 3-1, albeit with a different arrangement of the column positions.

```
SELECT PurchaseDate,
       StreetAddress,
       PaymentMethod,
       PurchasePrice,
       CustomerName
  FROM dbo.CustomerPurchaseInfo
```

Query 3-2

It is not necessary to select every column from the table. If only **PurchaseDate** and **PurchasePrice** were needed, **CustomerName**, **StreetAddress**, and **PaymentMethod** would be omitted from the query.

```
SELECT PurchaseDate,
       PurchasePrice
  FROM dbo.CustomerPurchaseInfo
```

Query 3-3

Query Results	
PurchaseDate	PurchasePrice
2020-04-12	53.4
2020-04-13	106.23
2020-04-17	82.11
2020-04-19	30.33
2020-04-23	87.93

Table 3-2

If a particular table has ten columns, and all ten columns need to be selected, it would be tedious to type the names of all of them. A shorthand way of selecting all columns is to use an asterisk, *.

```
SELECT *
  FROM dbo.CustomerPurchaseInfo
```

Query 3-4

This query returns the same results as Query 3-1, which had each column explicitly written out. Bear in mind that it is not considered good practice to use SELECT * when running large queries or operating on tables with many columns, especially when only one or two are required.

3.2 Distinct Values

Often, the individual rows in each column are less important than the overall composition of the column. Table 3-3 shows the entries in a sample table named *dbo.PurchaseDays*, representing the various days on which purchases were placed.

dbo.PurchaseDays	
PurchaseDate	PurchasePrice
2020-05-03	30.00
2020-05-01	25.00
2020-05-02	25.00
2020-05-05	35.00
2020-05-02	25.00
2020-05-02	20.00
2020-05-05	40.00
2020-05-03	35.00
2020-05-04	10.00
2020-05-02	10.00

Table 3-3

Suppose it is necessary to find out which days had purchases placed on them, irrespective of how many purchases there were on that day or how much the purchases were for. With this task in mind, it is not useful to know that there was one purchase made on the 1st for $25, four purchases made on the 2nd ranging from $10 to $25, etc.

SQL has the ability to select the unique (or in proper terminology, the *distinct*) values in a column. This is done by adding DISTINCT between SELECT and the first column in the list.

```
  SELECT
DISTINCT Columns
    FROM Table
```

Syntax 3-2

Query 3-5 shows how to use DISTINCT to find the unique values of **PurchaseDate**.

```
  SELECT
DISTINCT PurchaseDate
    FROM dbo.PurchaseDays
```

Query 3-5

Query Results
PurchaseDate
2020-05-03
2020-05-01
2020-05-02
2020-05-05
2020-05-04

Table 3-4

Query 3-5 can be extended to include multiple columns. If **PurchasePrice** is added to the column list, the result set will be every distinct combination of **PurchaseDate** and **PurchasePrice**.

```
   SELECT
DISTINCT PurchaseDate,
         PurchasePrice
   FROM dbo.PurchaseDays
```

Query 3-6

Query Results	
PurchaseDate	PurchasePrice
2020-05-03	30.00
2020-05-01	25.00
2020-05-02	25.00
2020-05-05	35.00
2020-05-02	20.00
2020-05-05	40.00
2020-05-03	35.00
2020-05-04	10.00
2020-05-02	10.00

Table 3-5

This is almost the same result set as Table 3-3, with the exception of one row. The original Table 3-3 had two rows with both a **PurchaseDate** of 2020-05-02 and a **PurchasePrice** of $25.00. Since all duplicates have been removed, one of the copies of the rows is not shown in the results.

3.3 Ordering Results

After executing a query, the results will be returned in whatever order they were entered in into the table originally. The results of a query can be sorted on one or more columns to fit the needs of the user. This is done by adding ORDER BY at the end of a query, followed by the columns by which the results will be sorted.

```
SELECT Columns
   FROM Table
ORDER BY Columns
```
Syntax 3-3

By default, columns are sorted in ascending order: alphabetically from A to Z, chronologically from earliest to latest, and numerically from lowest to highest. While not necessary (since it is the default), ascending order can be specified by adding the expression ASC after the column name in the ORDER BY clause. To sort the results in *descending* order, the expression DESC can be added after the column name (ORDER BY **Column** DESC).

Referring back to Table 3-3, the data can be sorted based on **PurchaseDate** by adding ORDER BY PurchaseDate as the last line of the query.

```
SELECT PurchaseDate,
       PurchasePrice
   FROM dbo.PurchaseDays
ORDER BY PurchaseDate
```
Query 3-7

Query Results	
PurchaseDate	PurchasePrice
2020-05-01	25.00
2020-05-02	25.00
2020-05-02	25.00
2020-05-02	20.00
2020-05-02	10.00
2020-05-03	30.00
2020-05-03	35.00
2020-05-04	10.00
2020-05-05	40.00
2020-05-05	35.00

Table 3-6

PurchaseDate has been sorted in ascending order, but **PurchasePrice** is still unsorted. SQL can sort by multiple columns if said columns are also listed in the ORDER BY clause, separated by commas. Query 3-8 shows how to retrieve the data from *dbo.PurchaseDays*, sorted by **PurchaseDate** first, and then by **PurchasePrice**.

```
    SELECT PurchaseDate,
           PurchasePrice
      FROM dbo.PurchaseDays
  ORDER BY PurchaseDate,
           PurchasePrice
```

Query 3-8

Query Results	
PurchaseDate	PurchasePrice
2020-05-01	25.00
2020-05-02	10.00
2020-05-02	20.00
2020-05-02	25.00
2020-05-02	25.00
2020-05-03	30.00
2020-05-03	35.00
2020-05-04	10.00
2020-05-05	35.00
2020-05-05	40.00

Table 3-7

The sorting directions of the columns do not need to be the same. They can be a mix of both ascending and descending order. The results can be sorted by **PurchaseDate** in ascending order, and then **PurchasePrice** in descending order, or vice versa.

SQL contains a shortcut to order columns. Instead of writing the full name of the columns in the ORDER BY clause, each column can be referenced by their positions within the column list. Query 3-8 can be rewritten to implement this shortcut.

```
    SELECT PurchaseDate,
           PurchasePrice
      FROM dbo.PurchaseDays
  ORDER BY 1,
           2
```

Query 3-9

In Query 3-9, 1 and 2 are used instead of **PurchaseDate** and **PurchasePrice**. The 1 refers to **PurchaseDate** because it is the first item in the list of columns. The same logic applies to **PurchasePrice**; it is the second item in the list of columns, and is referred to as 2. Both Query 3-8 and Query 3-9 will return the same data.

Be careful when using this method, though. If a new column were placed at the beginning of the list, column 1 would refer to this new column, and column 2 would refer to **PurchaseDate** (i.e., your original sorting would no longer apply).

3.4 Selecting Without a FROM Clause

It is not always necessary to have a FROM clause in a query[4]. Sometimes there are values that don't come from any table. The simplest example is directly selecting a value.

```
SELECT 1
```
Query 3-10

Query Results
(No column name)
1

Table 3-8

```
SELECT 'Hello world!'
```
Query 3-11

Query Results
(No column name)
Hello world!

Table 3-9

Multiple values can be selected by separating them with commas. Each value will become its own column in the result set.

```
SELECT 'My name is', 'Greg'
```
Query 3-12

Query Results	
(No column name)	(No column name)
My name is	Greg

Table 3-10

There are also functions that return dynamic values (a.k.a. *non-deterministic* functions). For example, GETDATE() will return the current date and time.

```
SELECT GETDATE()
```
Query 3-13

Query Results
(No column name)
2020-08-26 11:06:08.330

Table 3-11

More functions like GETDATE() can be found in Appendix B: Selected Functions. If you're not selecting a pre-existing column from a table, the resulting column will be given the title "(No column name)." This is normal, and will be touched on in a later chapter.

---

[4] Not every implementation of SQL allows you to omit a FROM clause. Literals, strings, integers, functions, etc. can still be selected, but they need to be selected from a "dummy" table. For example, in Oracle, this dummy table is named *Dual*, and in Db2, it's *SysIBM.SysDummy1*.

3.5   Commenting Out Code

Comments are SQL's way of saying "ignore this particular code" when running a query. They are useful for making changes to a query that can be easily reverted. Suppose we wanted to execute Query 3-1 with **StreetAddress** temporarily removed. Instead of deleting **StreetAddress**, two dashes can be placed in front of the column. This will tell SQL to ignore everything after the dashes on that particular line. If there is any text *before* the dashes on that line, it *will* be included in the query.

```
SELECT CustomerName,
       --StreetAddress,
       PurchaseDate,
       PurchasePrice,
       PaymentMethod
  FROM dbo.CustomerPurchaseInfo
```

Query 3-14

Query Results			
CustomerName	PurchaseDate	PurchasePrice	PaymentMethod
Gail Curran	2020-04-12	53.4	Credit card
Peter Gray	2020-04-13	106.23	Credit card
Nicholas Hill	2020-04-17	82.11	Cash
Julie Moss	2020-04-19	30.33	Cash
Lela Girard	2020-04-23	87.93	Credit card

Table 3-12

When **StreetAddress** must be reintroduced into the query, all that is needed to re-activate the code is to delete the two dashes.

Comments do not need to be made line-by-line. Visiting Query 3-1 once more, suppose we wanted to temporarily remove all columns except **CustomerName** and **PaymentMethod**. One way to do this is to individually comment each line, but that is an unnecessary amount of work.

SQL has the ability to create block-comments. This allows for any amount of code to be commented out without having to individually comment out each line. The start of a block-comment is signified by a forward-slash and then an asterisk, /*. The end of a block-comment is the opposite, an asterisk and then a forward-slash, */. Everything between the start and end of the block-comment will be ignored during execution.

```
SELECT CustomerName,
    /*
        StreetAddress,
        PurchaseDate,
        PurchasePrice,
    */
        PaymentMethod
  FROM dbo.CustomerPurchaseInfo
```

Query 3-15

Query Results	
CustomerName	PaymentMethod
Gail Curran	Credit card
Peter Gray	Credit card
Nicholas Hill	Cash
Julie Moss	Cash
Lela Girard	Credit card

Table 3-13

And to revert these changes, we need only delete the /* and the */.

3.6   Inserting Into Tables With a Select Statement

SQL offers several ways to insert data directly into a table using a `SELECT` statement; no manual listing of values required. The first of these is the `INSERT INTO—SELECT` method.

```
INSERT INTO Target Table
SELECT Columns
  FROM Source Table
```

Syntax 3-4

When using this syntax, SQL will execute the `SELECT—FROM` query and insert the results into the target table. This is useful for situations in which data exists in one table, and it must be copied into another table. With this type of `INSERT` statement, the target table must already exist before the query is executed.

The same restrictions apply to this method of insertion that apply to inserting rows as described in chapter 2.5; values must obey the definitions of the columns they are being inserted into, the number of items in the column list should match the number of columns in the target table, and the order of the selected columns should match the order of the columns in the target table (this can also be overridden by specifying the order of columns like in Query 2-4).

The second method of inserting into a table is to use `SELECT—INTO`.

```
SELECT Columns
  INTO Target Table
  FROM Source Table
```

Syntax 3-5

There is one major difference between these two methods of inserting data. When using `SELECT—INTO`, the target table must *not* exist before the query is executed. SQL will *create* a table based off of the results of the query. The data types of the columns in the new table will be set automatically.

3.7 Literal, Calculated, and Derived Columns

In chapter 3.4, we learned that we are not bound by the presence of a table to be able to return useful information in SQL. Going one step further, even if a table is present, we are not limited to the data that is in it. Additional columns (that don't already exist) can be placed in the column list of a query, and they can be and populated with whatever data we desire. These columns are temporary; they are calculated at run-time, displayed in the results, and then cease to exist.

3.7.1 Literal columns

In SQL terminology, a static value (a number, string of text, or date) is called a "literal." This means that 1, Hello world!, etc. are literals. I have modified Query 3-1 to also include a literal column.

```
SELECT 'Valued customer',
       CustomerName,
       StreetAddress,
       PurchaseDate,
       PurchasePrice,
       PaymentMethod
  FROM dbo.CustomerInformation
```
Query 3-16

Since I have specified what the value of the first column will be ("Valued customer"), this new column will be populated entirely by literal values. These are constant and do not depend on the data within the table.

Query Results					
(No column name)	CustomerName	StreetAddress	PurchaseDate	PurchasePrice	PaymentMethod
Valued customer	Gail Curran	3920 Arthur Rd	2020-04-12	53.4	Credit card
Valued customer	Peter Gray	2054 College Vw	2020-04-13	106.23	Credit card
Valued customer	Nicholas Hill	4427 Losh Ave	2020-04-17	82.11	Cash
Valued customer	Julie Moss	4506 Oliver Ave	2020-04-19	30.33	Cash
Valued customer	Lela Girard	3554 Stuart St	2020-04-23	87.93	Credit card

Table 3-14

3.7.2 Calculated Columns

Different functions can be performed on columns, which will temporarily alter their values. Consider the following table, which shows the names and exam grades of ten students.

dbo.ExamGrades	
Student	**Grade**
Gina Melvin	76
Donny Wilmoth	76
Barbara Fisher	99
John Fleck	77
Clayton Wheeler	88
Robert Harris	84
Kenneth Copeland	50
Christine Cox	33
Robert Ruhl	36
Billy Hill	49

Table 3-15

Imagine the teacher realized that she had made an error on the test, and as a result, she would like to award each student one extra point. To display this new information, we will select the information from the table as we normally would, except instead of displaying **Grade**, we'll display **Grade** + 1.

```
SELECT Student,
       Grade + 1
  FROM dbo.ExamGrades
```

Query 3-17

Query Results	
Student	**(No column name)**
Gina Melvin	77
Donny Wilmoth	77
Barbara Fisher	100
John Fleck	78
Clayton Wheeler	89
Robert Harris	85
Kenneth Copeland	51
Christine Cox	34
Robert Ruhl	37
Billy Hill	50

Table 3-16

Now the results reflect the new grades.

We are not limited to only mathematical functions. More functions (such as those that operate on text or dates) can be found in Appendix B: Selected Functions.

3.7.3   Ordering By Calculated Columns

Just because we can create a calculated column, doesn't mean we always want to select it in our final result set. Consider the table *dbo.MonthlySales*, which shows the total number of sales for each calendar month for another fictional company. In its current form, the data is in no particular order.

dbo.MonthlySales	
SalesMonth	**NumSales**
February 2020	275
August 2020	520
May 2020	430
March 2020	350
December 2020	290
September 2020	460
November 2020	320
January 2020	250
April 2020	380
July 2020	580
October 2020	400
June 2020	560

Table 3-17

Imagine that the table had accidentally been created with **SalesMonth** as a column of strings rather than dates. What implications does this have when it comes to manipulating data? What if someone wanted this data in chronological order? Since the column contains strings, if it were ordered by **SalesMonth**, the results would be sorted in *alphabetical* order.

Query Results	
SalesMonth	**NumSales**
April 2020	380
August 2020	520
December 2020	290
February 2020	275
January 2020	250
July 2020	580
June 2020	560
March 2020	350
May 2020	430
November 2020	320
October 2020	400
September 2020	460

Table 3-18

One possible method to sort it properly is to identify the number of the month that each **SalesMonth** corresponds to (e.g., January is month one, February is month two, etc.). Then, the data can be ordered based on that number.

The DATEPART function can be used to return the number of the month for a particular date(time). More information on the proper use of the DATEPART function can be found in Appendix B: Selected Functions.

```
    SELECT SalesMonth,
           NumSales,
           DATEPART(MONTH, SalesMonth)
      FROM dbo.MonthlySales
  ORDER BY DATEPART(MONTH, SalesMonth)
```

Query 3-18

Query Results		
SalesMonth	**NumSales**	(No column name)
January 2020	250	1
February 2020	275	2
March 2020	350	3
April 2020	380	4
May 2020	430	5
June 2020	560	6
July 2020	580	7
August 2020	520	8
September 2020	460	9
October 2020	400	10
November 2020	320	11
December 2020	290	12

Table 3-19

The data is now in chronological order, but there is a new problem, we don't need the third column. Thankfully, the column or expression that the data is ordered by *does not* need to be present in the column list. Query 3-18 can be modified to exclude the DATEPART function from the column list, while keeping it in the ORDER BY clause. This will produce the same result set as Table 3-19, but without the unnecessary third column.

This rule does not apply if DISTINCT is being utilized in the query. If it is, any columns that the results are ordered by *must* appear in the column list as well.

3.7.4 Case Statements

The CASE statement is SQL's equivalent of an IF—THEN—ELSE statement. If *a condition* is true (such as a column is equal to some value, or a column is greater than/less than some value), then return *a value*, or else return *a different value*. A CASE statement will display a new column whose value depends on the logic supplied.

```
SELECT CASE WHEN Condition
            THEN Some Value
            ELSE Other Value
              END
  FROM Table
```

Syntax 3-6

At least one WHEN/THEN pair is required, but multiple pairs are allowed. If the CASE statement contains multiple WHEN/THEN pairs, they must be placed sequentially. The ELSE expression (optional) is what the value of the column will default to if none of the earlier conditions are met. If the ELSE line is omitted and none of the conditions are met, the column will default to null for that row. The END expression concludes the CASE statement.

Returning to Table 3-15, we can add a column with a CASE statement to determine if the student passed or failed the test. If the student passed, the new column displays "Passed," or else it displays "Failed." The following code examples make use of the greater-than-or-equal-to operator. More details about this and other operators can be found in chapter 4.

```
SELECT Student,
       Grade,
       CASE WHEN Grade >= 60
            THEN 'Passed'
            ELSE 'Failed'
              END
  FROM dbo.ExamGrades
```

Query 3-19

Query Results		
Student	**Grade**	**(No column name)**
Gina Melvin	76	Passed
Donny Wilmoth	76	Passed
Barbara Fisher	99	Passed
John Fleck	77	Passed
Clayton Wheeler	88	Passed
Robert Harris	84	Passed
Kenneth Copeland	50	Failed
Christine Cox	33	Failed
Robert Ruhl	36	Failed
Billy Hill	49	Failed

Table 3-20

If a letter grade, A-F, is preferred over simply Passed and Failed, multiple WHEN/THEN statements can be utilized.

```
SELECT Student,
       Grade,
       CASE WHEN Grade >= 90 THEN 'A'
            WHEN Grade >= 80 AND Grade < 90 THEN 'B'
            WHEN Grade >= 70 AND Grade < 80 THEN 'C'
            WHEN Grade >= 60 AND Grade < 70 THEN 'D'
            ELSE 'F'
            END
  FROM dbo.ExamGrades
```

Query 3-20

Query Results		
Student	**Grade**	(No column name)
Gina Melvin	76	C
Donny Wilmoth	76	C
Barbara Fisher	99	A
John Fleck	77	C
Clayton Wheeler	88	B
Robert Harris	84	B
Kenneth Copeland	50	F
Christine Cox	33	F
Robert Ruhl	36	F
Billy Hill	49	F

Table 3-21

CASE statements are evaluated sequentially. SQL will evaluate the first WHEN condition. If the condition is *true*, SQL will follow through with the corresponding THEN statement. If the condition is *not* true, SQL will evaluate the next condition. As soon as a condition is met SQL follows through with the THEN statement, and the CASE statement will terminate for that row. Any following branches are not evaluated. The previous query can therefore be simplified.

```
SELECT Student,
       Grade,
       CASE WHEN Grade >= 90 THEN 'A'
            WHEN Grade >= 80 THEN 'B'
            WHEN Grade >= 70 THEN 'C'
            WHEN Grade >= 60 THEN 'D'
            ELSE 'F'
            END
  FROM dbo.ExamGrades
```

Query 3-21

If a student has a grade of 95, then technically they qualify for all of the conditions (as 95 is greater than 90, and greater than 80, and greater than 70, etc.). But since SQL stops executing the CASE statement once a condition is met, it will follow through with the THEN 'A' statement, and then terminate. If the grade were an 85 instead, it would fail to meet the first condition, but it *would* meet the second condition, follow through with the THEN 'B' statement, and then stop executing.

CASE statements can also be nested, meaning that they can be placed within one another. By nesting them, we can further break down the student's grades into + and − letter grades. For the sake of brevity, only the first letter grade will be shown.

38

```
SELECT Student,
       Grade,
       CASE WHEN Grade >= 90
               THEN CASE WHEN Grade >= 97 THEN 'A+'
                         WHEN Grade >= 94 THEN 'A'
                         WHEN Grade >= 90 THEN 'A-'
                            END
            END
  FROM dbo.ExamGrades
```

Query 3-22

When executing, SQL will first check to see if the grade is equal to or above 90. If it is, it will begin another CASE statement to check where in the 90s the grade falls. If the score is in the upper 90s, it returns A+, if it is in the mid-90s, it returns A, and if it is in the low-90s, it returns A-.

There is another way to implement a CASE statement. If a CASE statement only checks to see if one column is *equal to* another value, the syntax can be simplified. Other comparisons like less-than, less-than-or-equal-to, etc. are not allowed. Conditions that make use of AND and OR operators (chapter 4.1) are also not allowed.

```
SELECT CASE Column
            WHEN Value
            THEN Some Value
            ELSE Other Value
             END
  FROM Table
```

Syntax 3-7

The syntax for the simple CASE statement is different than the usual syntax. Syntax 3-7 would be executed *as if* it were written as follows.

```
SELECT CASE WHEN Column = Value
            THEN Some Value
            ELSE Other Value
             END
  FROM Table
```

Syntax 3-8

The advantage of this simpler style over the conventional style is that if there are multiple WHEN statements, the expression *column* = does not need to be written for every line. For example, the following two queries are identical in how they will execute, but they are written using the two different syntaxes. First, the typical way.

```
SELECT CASE WHEN Grade = 'A' THEN 'Amazing job, great effort!'
            WHEN Grade = 'B' THEN 'Keep up the good work!'
            WHEN Grade = 'C' THEN 'Study harder next time.'
            WHEN Grade = 'D' THEN 'Try harder or you will fail.'
            ELSE 'See me after class.'
             END
  FROM dbo.ExamGrades
```

Query 3-23

And next, the simple way.

```
SELECT CASE Grade
            WHEN 'A' THEN 'Amazing job, great effort!'
            WHEN 'B' THEN 'Keep up the good work!'
            WHEN 'C' THEN 'Study harder next time.'
            WHEN 'D' THEN 'Try harder or you will fail.'
            ELSE 'See me after class.'
             END
  FROM dbo.ExamGrades
```

Query 3-24

In Query 3-24, every WHEN statement is checking to see if **Grade** is equal to A, B, C, etc., even though it isn't explicitly written that way.

3.7.5 IIF Statements

The immediate-if (`IIF`) statement is another option for calculated columns which rely on true/false expressions, and is an additional shorthand way of writing a `CASE` statement.

```
SELECT Columns,
       IIF(Condition, Value If True, Value If False)
  FROM Table
```
Syntax 3-9

For readers familiar with Microsoft Excel, the `IIF` statement has the same syntax as Excel's IF statement; if some condition is true, then display a value, or else display another value. Query 3-19 can be recreated using an `IIF` statement.

```
SELECT Student,
       Grade,
       IIF(Grade >= 60, 'Passed', 'Failed')
  FROM dbo.ExamGrades
```
Query 3-25

The results from this query will be identical to Table 3-20.

`IIF` statements can be nested by placing another entire `IIF` statement within the **Value If False** expression of the main `IIF` function.

3.7.6 Window Functions and Partitioning

Back in chapter 3.7.3, we saw that a function normally will only accept the input from one row, and output one value. When scanning through *dbo.MonthlySales*, the DATEPART function only took in one value, **SalesMonth**, from the particular row that it was processing, and returned the number of the month, no matter what other values of **SalesMonth** were in the other rows. Window functions are a little different. Instead of accepting just one value, window functions can accept multiple values from multiple rows (within a "window" of rows), and then output a value. Later, in chapter 10.1, we'll explore some advanced features of window functions.

There are three popular window functions in SQL, ROW_NUMBER, RANK, and DENSE_RANK. These are ordinal functions, and each grant a position (1st, 2nd, 3rd, 4th, etc.) to a row based on how you choose to order the results. Compared to a typical function, they look different than what we've seen so far.

```
SELECT Columns,
       ROW_NUMBER() OVER (ORDER BY Columns),
       RANK()       OVER (ORDER BY Columns),
       DENSE_RANK() OVER (ORDER BY Columns)
  FROM Table
```
Syntax 3-10

Each function has an additional code snippet that says OVER (ORDER BY *Columns*). Naturally, with an *ordinal* function, we'd need something to order the rows by. If we had a table of employees, then perhaps we could calculate their position based on their salary. Table 3-22 will be the sample data set for this demonstration.

dbo.Employees	
EmployeeName	**Salary**
Gary Holman	70000
Derrick Horton	80000
Janis Alston	90000
Joann Mann	90000
Gerard Han	100000

Table 3-22

Each ordinal function[5] assigns values in a slightly different way:

- ROW_NUMBER provides an increasing numerical value for each row. In default ascending order, the employee with the lowest salary will have a row number of one. Even if two employees have the same salary, their row numbers will not be the same (but this is possible if they are partitioned, described shortly).

- RANK also provides an increasing number for each row, but it allows for two rows to have the same rank. If two employees have the same salary, they will have the same rank, and intermediate ranks will be skipped. E.g., if two employees are tied for second place, third place is skipped, and the next highest salary would be fourth place.

- DENSE_RANK is the same as RANK except that the intermediate ranks are not skipped.

---

[5] Unless given a new name, calculated columns will be given the default name of "(No column name)." However, in Table 3-23 and Table 3-24, I've made an exception. Since we're dealing with three new functions, I've chosen to simply add the names of the ordinal functions to the columns, so as not to confuse the reader. We will learn how to give names to columns in chapter 3.7.7.

The window in this scenario is the entire table. The entire table must be scanned, and then each row number/rank must be applied corresponding to where that row falls in relation to the other rows.

```
SELECT EmployeeName,
       Salary,
       ROW_NUMBER() OVER (ORDER BY Salary),
       RANK()       OVER (ORDER BY Salary),
       DENSE_RANK() OVER (ORDER BY Salary)
  FROM dbo.Employees
```

Query 3-26

EmployeeName	Salary	Row Number	Rank	Dense Rank
Gary Holman	70000	1	1	1
Derrick Horton	80000	2	2	2
Janis Alston	90000	3	3	3
Joann Mann	90000	4	3	3
Gerard Han	100000	5	5	4

Table 3-23

We also have the ability to break the data down into groups when applying the ordinal functions. This is known as *partitioning*. Assume that instead of ordering employees by just their salary, we wanted to order them by their salary within their respective departments. To achieve this, we will have to partition (or separate) the data by the department. Window functions can be partitioned by adding the phrase PARTITION BY *Columns* before ORDER BY.

```
SELECT Columns,
       ROW_NUMBER() OVER (PARTITION BY Columns ORDER BY Columns),
       RANK()       OVER (PARTITION BY Columns ORDER BY Columns),
       DENSE_RANK() OVER (PARTITION BY Columns ORDER BY Columns)
  FROM Table
```

Syntax 3-11

We'll assign Mr. Horton, Ms. Alston, and Ms. Mann to the billing department, Mr. Holman to the fulfillments department, and Mr. Han to the legal department. The billing, fulfillments, and legal departments will now each have their own highest paid employee, and their own lowest paid employee.

For the purposes of this exercise, we are going to reverse the ordering, so that instead of the lowest paid employee correspond to number one, the *highest* paid employee will be number one. Remember, to reverse the sorting order, DESC must be added after each column in the ORDER BY clause.

```
SELECT EmployeeName,
       Salary,
       Department,
       ROW_NUMBER() OVER (PARTITION BY Department ORDER BY Salary DESC),
       RANK()       OVER (PARTITION BY Department ORDER BY Salary DESC),
       DENSE_RANK() OVER (PARTITION BY Department ORDER BY Salary DESC)
  FROM dbo.Employees
```

Query 3-27

Query Results

EmployeeName	Salary	Department	Row Number	Rank	Dense Rank
Janis Alston	90000	Billing	1	1	1
Joann Mann	90000	Billing	2	1	1
Derrick Horton	80000	Billing	3	3	2
Gary Holman	70000	Fulfillments	1	1	1
Gerard Han	100000	Legal	1	1	1

Table 3-24

All of the row numbers and ranks are now relative to their respective departments. Compare Derrick Horton and Gary Holman. Derrick has a higher overall salary than Gary, yet he is ranked *lower* than Gary. This is because when the data is partitioned, SQL will only compare employees against other employees within the same department. Derrick and Gary are no longer compared to each other. Derrick is only compared to other people in the billing department. Each department has their own respective number one, who represents the highest paid employee.

3.7.7 Aliasing Columns

It was mentioned earlier, but if a query is executed that uses a calculated or derived column, the new column is given the heading "(No column name)." If you were to hand the results of the query to someone in a spreadsheet, how would they know what the column refers to?

SQL contains the ability to give tables and columns a temporary name. This is known as *aliasing*. Tables and columns are aliased by placing the phrase AS **Alias** after invoking it. The AS isn't strictly necessary, but it does help make the code easier to read. Referring back to the example from before about the exam with the one bonus point, the new column can be given the name **AdjustedGrade**.

```
SELECT Student,
       Grade + 1 AS AdjustedGrade
  FROM dbo.ExamGrades
```

Query 3-28

Query Results	
Student	**AdjustedGrade**
Gina Melvin	77
Donny Wilmoth	77
Barbara Fisher	100
John Fleck	78
Clayton Wheeler	89
Robert Harris	85
Kenneth Copeland	51
Christine Cox	34
Robert Ruhl	37
Billy Hill	50

Table 3-25

This is the same data as before, but now the column header shows that the column represents the adjusted grade of the student.

Aliases can be applied to any column, not just ones that are created at run-time. Quite often, tables will contain columns with abbreviated or very technical names (such as *dbo.TestTable* below) that should be aliased as a more natural term or name.

```
SELECT acctnum,
       straddr,
       dt_join,
       pnum
  FROM dbo.TestTable
```

Query 3-29

Query 3-29 would be better off having each column aliased with an easily understood name.

```
SELECT acctnum AS AccountNumber,
       straddr AS StreetAddress,
       dt_join AS JoinDate,
       pnum    AS PhoneNumber
  FROM dbo.TestTable
```

Query 3-30

When using only one table, aliasing is more a matter of convenience. It is not *necessary* to alias the table, but as we will see later when joining multiple tables together and using subqueries, aliasing may be necessary to clear up ambiguity and make the queries much easier to read and understand.

4 Choosing and Filtering Rows

4.1 Filtering Rows in the Results

By adding and removing items from the column list, we can choose only the columns that we want to display. But what if we wanted to filter the data to include only the *rows* that we want? This is done using a WHERE clause.

```
SELECT Columns
  FROM Table
 WHERE Condition
```
Syntax 4-1

Generally, the **condition** equates a column with a value. If that condition is true, the row is returned in the results. Going back to *dbo.CustomerPurchaseInfo*, what if we only wanted the rows where the customer made the purchase via a credit card?

```
SELECT CustomerName,
       StreetAddress,
       PurchaseDate,
       PurchasePrice,
       PaymentMethod
  FROM dbo.CustomerPurchaseInfo
 WHERE PaymentMethod = 'Credit card'
```
Query 4-1

Query Results				
CustomerName	StreetAddress	PurchaseDate	PurchasePrice	PaymentMethod
Gail Curran	3920 Arthur Rd	2020-04-12	53.4	Credit card
Peter Gray	2054 College Vw	2020-04-13	106.23	Credit card
Lela Girard	3554 Stuart St	2020-04-23	87.93	Credit card

Table 4-1

Query 4-1 returns only three out of the five rows in the table, because those three purchases used credit cards. In SQL Server, searches are case-*insensitive*. Running a query that searches for rows where **PaymentMethod** is equal to "Credit card" will return the same rows as a query that searches for "CREDIT CARD." This is not true for all SQL implementations though.

Filter conditions are not limited to two values being equal. It supports several common operators.

Comparison	Description
=	Equal to
!= or <>	Not equal to
>	Greater than
>=	Greater than or equal to
<	Less than
<=	Less than or equal to
BETWEEN x AND y	Between the values x and y

Table 4-2

Also, we are not limited to single conditions. By using the AND and OR operators, additional criteria can be entered.

```
SELECT CustomerName,
       StreetAddress,
       PurchaseDate,
       PurchasePrice,
       PaymentMethod
  FROM dbo.CustomerPurchaseInfo
 WHERE PurchasePrice < 60
    OR PurchaseDate = '2020-04-13'
```

Query 4-2

There are two criteria given in this query. In order for the row to be returned in the result set, the price has to be less than $60, or **PurchaseDate** has to be on the 13th of April.

CustomerName	StreetAddress	PurchaseDate	PurchasePrice	PaymentMethod
Gail Curran	3920 Arthur Rd	2020-04-12	53.4	Credit card
Peter Gray	2054 College Vw	2020-04-13	106.23	Credit card
Julie Moss	4506 Oliver Ave	2020-04-19	30.33	Cash

Query Results

Table 4-3

If the OR were switched to an AND and the query were executed, the result set would be empty. There are no rows that have *both* a purchase price under sixty dollars and a purchase date of the 13th. The two rows with a purchase price under sixty dollars occur on the 12th and 19th, and the only record that occurs on the 13th has a purchase price over sixty dollars.

Not all operators have the same precedence. For example, AND is evaluated before OR.

```
WHERE Condition A AND Condition B OR Condition C
```

This filter is evaluated as true if condition C is true, or *both* A and B are true. In order to force conditions to evaluate together, they can be wrapped together with parentheses, much like a mathematical statement.

```
WHERE Condition A AND (Condition B OR Condition C)
```

This filter is stating that in order for a row to be returned in the results, condition A must be true, and *either* B or C must be true.

4.2 Searching Between Two Values

Columns can be searched for values within a given range. The following WHERE clause offers one possible way to search for rows with a purchase date between April 17th, 2020 and April 20th, 2020.

```
WHERE PurchaseDate >= '2020-04-17'
  AND PurchaseDate <= '2020-04-20'
```

A better way to do this is by using the BETWEEN operator. This accomplishes the same goal, while eliminating the redundancy of writing **PurchaseDate** multiple times.

```
SELECT Columns
  FROM Table
WHERE Column BETWEEN 1st Value AND 2nd Value
```
Syntax 4-2

Query 4-3 shows the above example, modified to use BETWEEN.

```
SELECT CustomerName,
       StreetAddress,
       PurchaseDate,
       PurchasePrice,
       PaymentMethod
  FROM dbo.CustomerPurchaseInfo
 WHERE PurchaseDate BETWEEN '2020-04-17' AND '2020-04-20'
```
Query 4-3

The BETWEEN operator is *inclusive*, meaning that it includes the values specified in the search. This query will search for rows with dates of April 17th, 18th, 19th, and 20th.

| Query Results | | | | |
CustomerName	StreetAddress	PurchaseDate	PurchasePrice	PaymentMethod
Nicholas Hill	4427 Losh Ave	2020-04-17	82.11	Cash
Julie Moss	4506 Oliver Ave	2020-04-19	30.33	Cash

Table 4-4

BETWEEN is not limited to dates. It can be applied to numerical quantities as well. If we wanted to show the rows with a purchase price between $30 and $60, the WHERE clause in Query 4-3 would read:

```
WHERE PurchasePrice BETWEEN 30 AND 60
```

4.3 Negating Conditions With !=, <>, and NOT

The conditions in WHERE clauses can be negated by using the *not-equal-to* operator, != or <> (both are acceptable). To modify Query 4-1 to include only rows where the payment method was *not* a credit card, the WHERE clause would be changed to read WHERE PaymentMethod != 'Credit card'.

Query Results				
CustomerName	StreetAddress	PurchaseDate	PurchasePrice	PaymentMethod
Nicholas Hill	4427 Losh Ave	2020-04-17	82.11	Cash
Julie Moss	4506 Oliver Ave	2020-04-19	30.33	Cash

Table 4-5

It is also possible to negate comparisons by placing the word NOT *before* the condition. Another way to search for rows where the payment method was not a credit card is to modify the WHERE clause to read:

```
WHERE NOT PaymentMethod = 'Credit card'
```

Leveraging NOT can sometimes help simplify filter logic. The condition:

```
WHERE NOT Condition A AND NOT Condition B
```

is equivalent to:

```
WHERE NOT (Condition A OR Condition B)
```

And likewise:

```
WHERE NOT Condition A OR NOT Condition B
```

is equivalent to:

```
WHERE NOT (Condition A AND Condition B)
```

4.4 Searching for NULLs

Searching for null values within data is different than searching for values normally. A null value cannot be searched for by using the condition WHERE **Column** = NULL. SQL Server won't throw an error, but the results will not be correct. As a quick example, observe the following table, *dbo.IntegerTable*. It is nothing more than several integers, and some entries which are null.

dbo.IntegerTable
RandomInteger
5
NULL
3
2
NULL

Table 4-6

Query 4-4 was written to search for null values using the *incorrect* method described above.

```
SELECT RandomInteger
  FROM dbo.IntegerTable
 WHERE RandomInteger = NULL
```

Query 4-4

Query Results
RandomInteger

Table 4-7

The resulting data set will be empty, despite *dbo.IntegerTable* containing two null values. The correct syntax to search for null values is WHERE **Column** IS NULL. And conversely, to search for rows where the value is *not* null, the correct syntax is WHERE **Column** IS NOT NULL.

If Query 4-4 is rewritten to utilize the correct method of searching for nulls, the expected results are obtained.

```
SELECT RandomInteger
  FROM dbo.IntegerTable
 WHERE RandomInteger IS NULL
```

Query 4-5

Query Results
RandomInteger
NULL
NULL

Table 4-8

4.5 Searching For Values Within a List

There will be times when you are searching for several possible values within the same column. For example, you have a table named *dbo.CalendarDays* with every calendar date of 2020, and what day of the week it corresponds to (not all rows shown).

dbo.CalendarDays	
CalendarDate	**DayOfTheWeek**
2020-01-01	Wednesday
2020-01-02	Thursday
2020-01-03	Friday
2020-01-04	Saturday
2020-01-05	Sunday
2020-01-06	Monday
2020-01-07	Tuesday
2020-01-08	Wednesday
2020-01-09	Thursday
2020-01-10	Friday
Etc.	

Table 4-9

If you want to search for all days which are weekdays (Monday through Friday), one possibility is the following.

```
SELECT CalendarDate,
       DayOfTheWeek
  FROM dbo.CalendarDays
 WHERE DayOfTheWeek = 'Monday'
    OR DayOfTheWeek = 'Tuesday'
    OR DayOfTheWeek = 'Wednesday'
    OR DayOfTheWeek = 'Thursday'
    OR DayOfTheWeek = 'Friday'
```

Query 4-6

But it is awfully verbose to write `DayOfTheWeek = ...` OR five times. Instead, we can utilize an `IN` list. An `IN` list will allow us to equate one column (**DayOfTheWeek**) to multiple values (Monday, Tuesday, etc.) without writing `DayOfTheWeek = ...` OR multiple times.

```
SELECT Columns
  FROM Table
 WHERE Column IN (Values)
```

Syntax 4-3

The values inside the parentheses should be separated by commas, and should also match the data type of the column they are being compared against.

```
SELECT CalendarDate,
       DayOfTheWeek
  FROM dbo.CalendarDays
 WHERE DayOfTheWeek IN ('Monday',
                        'Tuesday',
                        'Wednesday',
                        'Thursday',
                        'Friday')
```

Query 4-7

Query Results	
CalendarDate	**DayOfTheWeek**
2020-01-01	Wednesday
2020-01-02	Thursday
2020-01-03	Friday
2020-01-06	Monday
2020-01-07	Tuesday
2020-01-08	Wednesday
2020-01-09	Thursday
2020-01-10	Friday
Etc.	

Table 4-10

Lists such as these can also be negated by placing NOT in front of IN. This will have the effect of searching for values of **DayOfTheWeek** which are *not* present within the list of values (Saturday and Sunday).

4.6   Searching for Approximate Matches

We don't always want to search for exact matches. Sometimes it's desirable to search for approximate matches. Returning to *dbo.CustomerPurchaseInfo*, if we want to search for everyone whose street address contains the phrase "ave" somewhere within it, we will use the LIKE operator in conjunction with the wildcard character, %. The wildcard character, when used within a search, tells SQL that there can be *any character, and any number of characters* (including none) in that position.

```
SELECT CustomerName,
       StreetAddress,
       PurchaseDate,
       PurchasePrice,
       PaymentMethod
  FROM dbo.CustomerPurchaseInfo
 WHERE StreetAddress LIKE '%ave%'
```

Query 4-8

Query Results				
CustomerName	StreetAddress	PurchaseDate	PurchasePrice	PaymentMethod
Nicholas Hill	4427 Losh Ave	2020-04-17	82.11	Cash
Julie Moss	4506 Oliver Ave	2020-04-19	30.33	Cash

Table 4-11

Surrounding "ave" with %s on both sides means that the phrase can appear at the start, at the end, or anywhere in the middle of the **StreetAddress** value. Placing a % *before* "ave" only would search for rows where "ave" appears at the end of the value (since any characters can appear before it). The opposite is also true. If a % is placed *after* the expression only, SQL will only search for rows where "ave" appears at the *start* of the value.

Approximate matches can also be negated with the NOT expression.

```
SELECT CustomerName,
       StreetAddress,
       PurchaseDate,
       PurchasePrice,
       PaymentMethod
  FROM dbo.CustomerPurchaseInfo
 WHERE StreetAddress NOT LIKE '%ave%'
```

Query 4-9

Query Results				
CustomerName	StreetAddress	PurchaseDate	PurchasePrice	PaymentMethod
Gail Curran	3920 Arthur Rd	2020-04-12	53.4	Credit card
Peter Gray	2054 College Vw	2020-04-13	106.23	Credit card
Lela Girard	3554 Stuart St	2020-04-23	87.93	Credit card

Table 4-12

Since the % wildcard allows for any number of characters, if you were to search within a table of customer names with the condition WHERE LastName LIKE '%son', the results would be of varying length; Edison, Johnson, Jackson, Ryerson, Paulson, Samson, etc. This does not allow searching for, say, values that only have four characters before "son."

SQL has implemented this search feature with the single-character wildcard, the underscore, _. The single-character wildcard allows for any *one* character in the given position, rather than the unlimited amount (or none) that the regular wildcard % allows. If the query included the condition `WHERE LastName LIKE '_ _ _ _son'` (spaces added between wildcards for clarity) only last names that end in "son" and have four characters before it would be present in the results. In contrast to %son, _ _ _ _son would only return Johnson, Jackson, Ryerson, and Paulson. Edison and Samson would be excluded because those have only three characters before "son."

One last point to make before moving on, if you use a wildcard without using `LIKE`, you will simply be searching for the literal wildcard characters.

4.6.1   Further Options for Approximate Matches

The two wildcards, `%` and `_`, should serve you well for most of what you'll likely need, but there is always the possibility that you'll need some further flexibility for very specific searches.

The first option is the range and set wildcard, `[` and `]`. In between the brackets, you may specify a range of possible values, or a set of specific values that you want to search for. For example, if you search through a list of words in the English language using the condition `WHERE word LIKE '[f-m]ellow'`, SQL will search for words that begin with the letters between (and including) "f" and "m," which are followed by "ellow." The word "bellow," for example, would not appear in the results, because the letter "b" is outside of the range.

The alternative is to use a set, such as `WHERE word LIKE '[bfm]ellow'`. This will search for words that begin with either "b," "f," or "m," which are followed by "ellow." This option *would* return the word "bellow," as we specified that the word may start with a "b."

Ranges and sets can be negated using the caret symbol, `^`. In our previous example, we could instead search for words that end in "ellow," but *do not* start with "f." This would be done by writing `WHERE word LIKE '[^f]ellow'`. Using the condition `WHERE word LIKE '[^b-m]ellow'` would have the effect of searching for words that end in "ellow," but start with a letter outside of the range of "b" through "m."

Numbers can also be entered into a range or set wildcard. Consider the following scenario: you work at a car manufacturer, and need the serial numbers for all cars of a specific model. The only way to differentiate one particular model from other models is that the first digit of the serial number is a number between 3 and 7, and the second is a 2 or 4. Anything after the first two digits doesn't matter. The proper SQL code for this search would be `WHERE serial LIKE '[3-7][24]%'`.

Escape characters are an important tool in searching for strings. In the world of coding, an escape character tells the program that the next character in the sequence isn't handled how it might normally be. Consider this scenario: you are searching through a column in a table for values such as `5%a`, `5%b`, `5%c`, `5%d`, and so on. The `%`s in these strings do *not* represent wildcards, they are just regular percent signs.

How might we search for these? You could say `WHERE Column = '5%a' OR Column = '5%b'`…, but that is a very verbose solution, and would be better suited as a range wildcard `[a-z]`. This would make it necessary to switch to `LIKE` instead of equals; `WHERE Column LIKE '5%[a-z]'`. You might see the problem with this approach. Once you switch to `LIKE` instead of equals, those percent signs become wildcards, not literal characters.

The solution is to *escape* the percent sign. Escaping it will tell SQL that the `%` is supposed to be interpreted as a literal character, not a wildcard. To escape something, we can choose an escape character at random; I'll choose the exclamation mark, `!`. The escape character precedes the percent sign, making our search term `'5!%[a-z]'`. After the search term, we must inform SQL that the exclamation mark is the escape character. This is done by adding the term:

ESCAPE ***Character***

Syntax 4-4

This would make our entire condition `WHERE Column LIKE '5!%[a-z]' ESCAPE '!'`

Even though the search term includes the exclamation mark, the mark isn't actually searched for. *It only tells SQL that the character after it is interpreted literally.* We can even escape characters with themselves. To search for exclamation marks, we could search for rows `WHERE Column LIKE '!!' ESCAPE '!'`, where the first exclamation mark only serves to tell SQL that the *next* exclamation mark is *not* an escape character.

4.7 Displaying Only a Certain Number of Rows

Depending on how many rows are in a table, it may not make sense for a query to retrieve every row from the table, especially if the table contains many rows. This is where TOP is useful. Using it, you can instruct SQL to only return a certain number, *N*, of rows (Syntax 4-5), or a certain percentage, *P*, of rows (Syntax 4-6).

```
SELECT
  TOP N Columns
    FROM Table
```

Syntax 4-5

```
SELECT
  TOP P
PERCENT Columns
    FROM Table
```

Syntax 4-6

In its current form, selecting the top rows will return the data in the order in which it was originally entered into the table. TOP can be used in conjunction with ORDER BY to gather some useful information. When using both together, the data will first be ordered by the given columns, and then the top rows from it will be selected. Returning to the exam grade scenario in chapter 3.7.2, we can easily find the five lowest-performing students.

```
SELECT
  TOP 5 Student,
        Grade
    FROM dbo.ExamGrades
ORDER BY Grade
```

Query 4-10

dbo.ExamGrades	
Student	**Grade**
Christine Cox	33
Robert Ruhl	36
Billy Hill	49
Kenneth Copeland	50
Gina Melvin	76

Table 4-13

4.7.1 Displaying the Top Rows With Ties

Imagine the same scenario, we have a list of student grades, and we want to find the top five students by score (this time with the highest score listed first). Here is the raw data again.

dbo.ExamGrades	
Student	**Grade**
Gina Melvin	76
Donny Wilmoth	76
Barbara Fisher	99
John Fleck	77
Clayton Wheeler	88
Robert Harris	84
Kenneth Copeland	50
Christine Cox	33
Robert Ruhl	36
Billy Hill	49

Table 4-14

If Query 4-10 is used in descending order, SQL will first order the data.

Query Results	
Student	**Grade**
Barbara Fisher	99
Clayton Wheeler	88
Robert Harris	84
John Fleck	77
Gina Melvin	76
Donny Wilmoth	76
Kenneth Copeland	50
Billy Hill	49
Robert Ruhl	36
Christine Cox	33

Table 4-15

Then it will select the top five rows.

Query Results	
Student	**Grade**
Barbara Fisher	99
Clayton Wheeler	88
Robert Harris	84
John Fleck	77
Gina Melvin	76

Table 4-16

Case closed, right? Not entirely. The goal was to find the top five students by score. If each student had a unique score, then this query would satisfy our needs, but both Donny Wilmoth and Gina Melvin have the same score. Technically both students should appear in the results. This is where using TOP by itself is insufficient; it only pulls rows based on the number of the row, not the value within the row.

There is an optional addition to TOP, known as WITH TIES. When implemented in Query 4-10, TOP WITH TIES will retrieve the first five rows based on the columns chosen in the ORDER BY clause (the exam grade), plus any additional rows whose grade is tied for last place (meaning that if we select the top 5 students with ties, we'd end up selecting the five highest scores, plus anyone else whose score is tied with fifth place). The syntax is similar to using just TOP, except after supplying the number of rows or percentage, you specify WITH TIES before the first column.

```
    SELECT
     TOP N
WITH TIES Columns
      FROM Table
  ORDER BY Columns
```

Syntax 4-7

```
    SELECT
     TOP P
   PERCENT
WITH TIES Columns
      FROM Table
  ORDER BY Columns
```

Syntax 4-8

If you are using TOP WITH TIES, you *must* have an ORDER BY clause, unlike the regular TOP which does not require it. If we modify the earlier query to select the top five students *with ties* ordered by grade, we get a different set of results.

Query Results	
Student	**Grade**
Barbara Fisher	99
Clayton Wheeler	88
Robert Harris	84
John Fleck	77
Gina Melvin	76
Donny Wilmoth	76

Table 4-17

4.8 Offsetting Results

We've learned so far that it is possible to select the top rows of a table, while ignoring the rest. The opposite is also true, we can ignore the top rows of a table and select the rest. This is done using the OFFSET clause.

```
   SELECT Columns
     FROM Table
 ORDER BY Columns
   OFFSET N ROWS
```

Syntax 4-9

The last line, OFFSET N ROWS, informs SQL of how many rows to skip when displaying the results of the query.

Returning to Query 4-10, we will remove the TOP 5 statement for now, and after the ORDER BY clause, we'll enter the line OFFSET 5 ROWS and execute the query.

```
   SELECT Student,
          Grade
     FROM dbo.ExamGrades
 ORDER BY Grade DESC
   OFFSET 5 ROWS
```

Query 4-11

Query Results	
Student	**Grade**
Donny Wilmoth	76
Kenneth Copeland	50
Billy Hill	49
Robert Ruhl	36
Christine Cox	33

Table 4-18

The results of the query show that the first five rows have been skipped, and the remainder of the table has been displayed. An OFFSET clause requires an ORDER BY clause. Without it, the query will not run.

4.8.1 Fetching Top Rows Using Offset

When using an OFFSET, the query *cannot* include TOP. This poses a problem. How can we select only the top portion of an offset record set? The solution is to use FETCH.

```
  SELECT Columns
    FROM Table
ORDER BY Columns
  OFFSET N ROWS
   FETCH FIRST J ROWS ONLY
```

Syntax 4-10

The line FETCH FIRST J ROWS ONLY informs SQL of how many rows[6] to retrieve after skipping the first N rows. Now we will modify Query 4-11 to fetch only the first three rows after the offset.

```
  SELECT Student,
         Grade
    FROM dbo.ExamGrades
ORDER BY Grade DESC
  OFFSET 5 ROWS
   FETCH FIRST 3 ROWS ONLY
```

Query 4-12

Query Results	
Student	Grade
Donny Wilmoth	76
Kenneth Copeland	50
Billy Hill	49

Table 4-19

Whereas Table 4-18 was the result of skipping five rows and then selecting the remainder of the table, Table 4-19 was the result of skipping five rows, and then selecting only the first three rows of the remainder.

---

[6] For the grammatically minded readers out there, you may have noticed that if you are only fetching a single row, the code would end up saying FETCH FIRST 1 ROWS ONLY, which is grammatically incorrect. The word ROWS may be substituted with ROW, and the query will function identically.

5 Aggregating Data

Individual rows are useful for showing individual pieces of information, but we may want to view aggregated data such as the sum of the values in a particular column, the maximum value, minimum value, etc. SQL has several built-in functions to aggregate data and return statistical calculations. The basis for an aggregated query is shown below.

```
SELECT Aggregate Function(Column)
  FROM Table
```

Syntax 5-1

For example, what if we wanted to calculate the sum of all money spent by customers at a particular clothing store over the course of time? Imagine we have a table called *dbo.Purchases* (Table 5-1) which contains four columns, **AccountNumber**, **PurchasePrice**, **PurchaseMonth**, and **CustomerState**.

dbo.Purchases			
AccountNumber	PurchasePrice	PurchaseMonth	CustomerState
241575	384.46	9	NY
241575	324.66	1	NY
471783	170.96	9	WI
471783	136.19	3	WI
589029	259.77	7	FL
589029	382.70	11	FL
871948	157.83	11	AK
871948	209.92	8	AK
986543	222.01	6	NC
986543	271.95	12	NC

Table 5-1

To find the total amount of money spent at the store, we will use the SUM function applied to **PurchasePrice**. This will perform $384.46 + $324.66 + $170.96 + etc. and return a single value.

```
SELECT SUM(PurchasePrice)
  FROM dbo.Purchases
```

Query 5-1

Query Results
(No column name)
2520.45

Table 5-2

There are more functions available than just SUM. MAX, MIN, and AVG are three additional functions which will calculate the maximum value, minimum value, and average value of a particular column, respectively. More aggregate functions can be found in Appendix B: Selected Functions.

5.1 Grouping Data

Query 5-1 will perform one sweeping calculation across the entire table. SQL is ignoring the values in the other columns when calculating the sum. But what if we needed to calculate the sum of **PurchasePrice** *for each unique customer?* The purchase prices for any two rows should only be added together if both have the same account number, i.e., they must be *grouped* together by their respective account numbers (this is the same concept as partitioning).

The values inside a column are grouped together by adding the term GROUP BY *Columns* after FROM.

```
SELECT Columns,
       Aggregate Function(Column)
  FROM Table
GROUP BY Columns
```

Syntax 5-2

From the example above about grouping by the account number:

```
SELECT AccountNumber,
       SUM(PurchasePrice)
  FROM dbo.Purchases
GROUP BY AccountNumber
```

Query 5-2

Query Results	
AccountNumber	(No column name)
241575	709.12
471783	307.15
589029	642.47
871948	367.75
986543	493.96

Table 5-3

If we wanted to know how much was spent in each month:

```
SELECT PurchaseMonth,
       SUM(PurchasePrice)
  FROM dbo.Purchases
GROUP BY PurchaseMonth
```

Query 5-3

Query Results	
PurchaseMonth	(No column name)
1	324.66
3	136.19
6	222.01
7	259.77
8	209.92
9	555.42
11	540.53
12	271.95

Table 5-4

Columns (excluding literal columns) that are not in the GROUP BY clause cannot be selected. Attempting to do so will result in an error from SQL. Any number of aggregate functions are allowed in a query. In addition to the sum of purchase prices, assume we wanted to find the earliest purchase month per customer as well as the least expensive purchase they've ever made.

```
SELECT AccountNumber,
       SUM(PurchasePrice),
       MIN(PurchaseMonth),
       MIN(PurchasePrice)
  FROM dbo.Purchases
GROUP BY AccountNumber
```

Query 5-4

Query Results			
AccountNumber	(No column name)	(No column name)	(No column name)
241575	709.12	1	324.66
471783	307.15	3	136.19
589029	642.47	7	259.77
871948	367.75	8	157.83
986543	493.96	6	222.01

Table 5-5

Another useful aggregate function is COUNT. The COUNT function will indicate how many rows belong to a particular group. COUNT does *not* require that a column be named inside its parentheses, and an asterisk can be used instead.

```
   SELECT AccountNumber,
          COUNT(*)
     FROM dbo.Purchases
 GROUP BY AccountNumber
```

Query 5-5

Query Results	
AccountNumber	(No column name)
241575	2
471783	2
589029	2
871948	2
986543	2

Table 5-6

Since each customer has two purchases, the COUNT function will return two for every row. By itself, it is a useful function, but the parameters inside the parentheses can be changed to give us more leverage in finding out useful information about a table.

For each group in the query results:
- COUNT(*) will count how many rows belong to the group, regardless of the value.
- COUNT(***Column***) will count how many rows in ***column*** contain values that are *not* null.
- COUNT(DISTINCT ***Column***) will count how many *distinct* values are present in ***column*** which are *not* null.

For example, in *dbo.Purchases*, every customer has two rows, and therefore, two **CustomerState** values (these two values are always identical for each customer, but there are two values nonetheless). To find out how many *distinct* values of **CustomerState** there are for each customer, use COUNT(DISTINCT CustomerState) instead of COUNT(*). Since each customer has only one unique value for **CustomerState**, the count of distinct states for each customer will be one. If a customer had placed a purchase, then moved to a different state and made another purchase, that particular customer would have a distinct count of two.

```
   SELECT AccountNumber,
          COUNT(DISTINCT CustomerState)
     FROM dbo.Purchases
 GROUP BY AccountNumber
```

Query 5-6

Query Results	
AccountNumber	(No column name)
241575	1
471783	1
589029	1
871948	1
986543	1

Table 5-7

It is possible to calculate grouped aggregate values (like those shown in Table 5-3 through Table 5-7) without having a GROUP BY statement. This will be explored further in chapter 10.1.

5.2 Filtering Aggregated Data

Like with any other data, we may want to filter it. Consider the following scenario. For the holidays, the same clothing store wants to send a free 25% off coupon to all of their customers who have spent $500 or more at their stores. How would a list of these customers be generated?

```
  SELECT AccountNumber,
         SUM(PurchasePrice)
    FROM dbo.Purchases
GROUP BY AccountNumber
   WHERE SUM(PurchasePrice) >= 500
```

Query 5-7

This would seem like the intuitive way to do it, but SQL differentiates between filtering on aggregated data, and filtering on *non*-aggregated data. The WHERE clause is only valid for data that has not been aggregated, while the sum of **PurchasePrice** is considered aggregated data. To filter aggregated data, the HAVING clause needs to be used. The HAVING clause is placed immediately after the GROUP BY clause.

```
  SELECT AccountNumber,
         SUM(PurchasePrice)
    FROM dbo.Purchases
GROUP BY AccountNumber
  HAVING SUM(PurchasePrice) >= 500
```

Query 5-8

Query Results	
AccountNumber	(No column name)
241575	709.12
589029	642.47

Table 5-8

Next, suppose that due to local laws, the state of Florida does not allow 25% off coupons, so they must be excluded from the query. What would the query be now?

```
  SELECT AccountNumber,
         SUM(PurchasePrice)
    FROM dbo.Purchases
GROUP BY AccountNumber
  HAVING SUM(PurchasePrice) >= 500
     AND CustomerState != 'FL'
```

Query 5-9

This would also be incorrect, since the HAVING clause only filters out aggregated data. The customer's home state is not a piece of aggregated data. The state, therefore, belongs in the WHERE clause. The filtering performed by the WHERE clause is carried out before the GROUP BY clause. SQL will first remove any row where **CustomerState** is equal to "FL." It will then group the remainder, sum the purchase prices, and *then* it will filter on the sum.

```
   SELECT AccountNumber,
          SUM(PurchasePrice)
     FROM dbo.Purchases
    WHERE CustomerState != 'FL'
 GROUP BY AccountNumber
   HAVING SUM(PurchasePrice) >= 500
```

Query 5-10

Query Results	
AccountNumber	(No column name)
241575	709.12

Table 5-9

Compared to Table 5-8, Table 5-9 has one fewer result. This is because account number 589029 resides in Florida, and was filtered out prior to aggregation.

6 Subqueries

6.1 General Structure and Aliasing

We will return to the example of a teacher who awards students extra points on their exam due to an error in one of the questions, only this time, she awards them ten extra points instead of only one.

```
SELECT Student,
       Grade + 10 AS NewGrade
  FROM dbo.ExamGrades
```

Query 6-1

With these new grades, she wants to know how many students scored a passing grade (above or equal to a 60).

```
SELECT Student,
       Grade + 10 AS NewGrade
  FROM dbo.ExamGrades
 WHERE NewGrade >= 60
```

Query 6-2

If executed, this query would not work, and SQL would return an error saying that it does not know what **NewGrade** is. This is due to the order of execution of different parts of a query. The filtering imposed by the WHERE clause is one of the first things to be processed by the query engine when running a query. The aliases on the columns are some of the *last* things to be applied by the query engine.

SQL begins the execution by attempting to reference a column which won't exist for a few more steps, which is why it fails. This same concept applies to the HAVING clause; we cannot filter on aliases (however, the ORDER BY clause is evaluated *after* the aliases are applied, so you *can* refer to columns by their aliases when sorting the results of a query). There are two ways to work around filtering on aliases. The first is by using the definition of the column instead of the alias.

```
SELECT Student,
       Grade + 10 AS NewGrade
  FROM dbo.ExamGrades
 WHERE Grade + 10 >= 60
```

Query 6-3

Query Results	
Student	Grade
Gina Melvin	86
Donny Wilmoth	86
Barbara Fisher	109
John Fleck	87
Clayton Wheeler	98
Robert Harris	94
Kenneth Copeland	60

Table 6-1

This isn't always the best method though. The definition of **NewGrade** was simple, `Grade + 10`, so placing the definition right into the `WHERE` clause didn't clutter the query up. What if the definition of **NewGrade** was something more complicated, like a lengthy `CASE` statement? If this were so, the *entire* `CASE` statement would need to be placed inside the `WHERE` clause, making the query long, and difficult to read. Furthermore, some functions won't even work with this method. Window functions like `ROW_NUMBER`, `RANK`, and `DENSE_RANK` (chapter 3.7.6) cannot be filtered on inside a `WHERE` clause (e.g., you cannot write `WHERE ROW_NUMBER() OVER ...`)[7].

Up to now, when selecting from tables, we've only been selecting from the original copy of them. Instead of selecting directly from the original copy, it is possible to select from a temporary version of it that has the aliases pre-applied to the columns. This allows for referencing columns by the chosen aliases rather than the logic used to calculate them. To accomplish this, we will be making a subquery.

To make a subquery, instead of writing `FROM` **Table** as you normally would, the *table* will be replaced with another query. The whole subquery needs to be surrounded by parentheses and aliased.

```
SELECT Column Aliases
  FROM (
          SELECT Columns AS Column Aliases
            FROM Table
       ) AS Subquery Alias
```

Syntax 6-1

If a query contains a subquery within it, the subquery will be executed first. The subquery will generate its own intermediary table of results. This table is then used by the main, or "outer" query. If the subquery had given any columns an alias, those aliases are "locked in," and the outer query can reference them. Likewise, any columns you create (such as calculated, literal, or `CASE` statement columns) *must* be given an alias. Returning to Query 6-2, it can be made to function as intended by utilizing a subquery.

```
SELECT Student,
       NewGrade
  FROM (
         SELECT Student,
                Grade + 10 AS NewGrade
           FROM dbo.ExamGrades
       ) AS s
 WHERE NewGrade >= 60
```

Query 6-4

In this example, the subquery calculates **Grade** + 10 for each student and applies the alias **NewGrade** to it, but does not perform any filtering. Once all students have been given a new grade, the subquery is finished processing, and is given the alias of s. The results are then passed to the outer query, where the filtering can take place, based on the alias **NewGrade**.

---

[7] Teradata *does* have the ability to perform such filtering by using the `QUALIFY` clause. In my opinion, this is one of the few significant advantages of Teradata over SQL Server.

6.2 Uncorrelated Subqueries

With our primer on aliasing subqueries, we can move on to uncorrelated subqueries. We will continue with the example of students and their exam grades. For sake of ease, we will be referring only to their original grades before any additional bonus points.

The next task will be to find the students who scored above the average of the class. Since we're filtering data, we're going to be using the WHERE clause. But how can we get the average of the class (an aggregated piece of data) and apply it to the WHERE clause? It turns out that not only can tables be replaced with subqueries, but *values* can be replaced with subqueries as well.

```
SELECT Student,
       Grade
  FROM dbo.ExamGrades
 WHERE Grade > (SELECT AVG(Grade)
                  FROM dbo.ExamGrades)
```

Query 6-5

Query Results	
Student	**Grade**
Gina Melvin	76
Donny Wilmoth	76
Barbara Fisher	99
John Fleck	77
Clayton Wheeler	88
Robert Harris	84

Table 6-2

In this instance, the subquery does not need to be aliased because it is not acting as a new table, it is only acting as a value for comparison purposes. In Query 6-5, the subquery only generates one value (the average of the score column), to which **Grade** is being compared. If the value for **Grade** from the outer query is greater than the average value, the row will be present in the results.

Consider the following scenario. The clothing company from chapter 3.1 is curious about how their stores are performing in sales. They have access to two tables, *dbo.StoreInformation*, which records each store number, the number of sales made at the store, as well as what US state the store is in. They also have access to a table named *dbo.RegionInformation* which contains all of the US states, and which region of the country that state belongs to (North-East, West, Midwest, and South).

dbo.StoreInformation				dbo.RegionInformation	
StoreNumber	**Sales**	**StoreState**		**US_State**	**Region**
3853	991	California		Alabama	South
1559	368	New York		Alaska	West
1410	862	Kansas		Arizona	West
0339	122	Oklahoma		Arkansas	South
7668	423	Oregon		California	West
Etc.				Etc.	

Table 6-3 and Table 6-4

To start, they want to see how the North-East is performing. One way they could accomplish this is to write:

```
SELECT StoreNumber,
       Sales
  FROM dbo.StoreInformation
 WHERE StoreState IN ('New York',
                      'Connecticut',
                      'Pennsylvania',
                      'Rhode Island',
                      etc.)
```
Query 6-6

But this is another verbose solution. The North-East region has nine states, meaning that nine lines will have to be written inside the parentheses. On top of this, every time you wish to change the region, you'd need to delete everything you've written and replace it with the new states. A more elegant solution would be to utilize a subquery within an IN list.

```
SELECT StoreNumber,
       NumberOfSales
  FROM dbo.StoreInformation
 WHERE StoreState IN (SELECT US_State
                        FROM RegionInformation
                       WHERE Region = 'North-East')
```
Query 6-7

The subquery will return a single column of values containing all of the states which are part of the North-East. SQL will only keep the rows from *dbo.StoreInformation* whose value for **StoreState** exists within that list. When using an IN list with a subquery, if the subquery returns more than one column, SQL will return an error.

While it was not used in the prior examples, subqueries can make use of TOP and ORDER BY. For example, if the subquery in Query 6-7 had used TOP 5 and ORDER BY US_State, it would have only generated a list containing the first five states from the North-East, sorted alphabetically, which would have changed the results of the overall query. Normally we'd get all of the sales for the stores in each of the nine states, but since we limited it to only five states, we'd return fewer results.

This chapter is named "uncorrelated subqueries." What is uncorrelated about these? They are named so because the information that is being returned in the subquery is in no way affected by the values in outer query; i.e., they are *not correlated*.

6.3 Correlated Subqueries

That begs the question, what is a *correlated* subquery? Simply put, it's a subquery whose values are dependent upon the values passed to it from the outer query. We will expand on the exam grades scenario. The exam grades table still refers to students who are all in the same class and taking the same test, but now the table also includes the school year (freshman, sophomore, junior, and senior) of the student who is taking the exam.

dbo.ExamGrades		
Student	**Grade**	**SchoolYear**
Gina Melvin	76	Freshman
Donny Wilmoth	76	Junior
Barbara Fisher	99	Sophomore
John Fleck	77	Senior
Clayton Wheeler	88	Sophomore
Robert Harris	84	Freshman
Kenneth Copeland	50	Freshman
Christine Cox	33	Senior
Robert Ruhl	36	Sophomore
Billy Hill	49	Junior

Table 6-5

Once more, we want to return the names and grades of students who performed better than the class average. Only this time, we want students who performed better than the average of all students *in the same school year*.

```
SELECT Student,
       Grade,
       SchoolYear
  FROM dbo.ExamGrades AS a
 WHERE Grade > (SELECT AVG(Grade)
                  FROM dbo.ExamGrades AS b
                 WHERE b.SchoolYear = a.SchoolYear)
```

Query 6-8

This query isn't quite like anything we've seen before. For starters, I've aliased tables instead of columns. Aliasing tables is a very commonly used and useful feature, and allows you to refer to ambiguous columns. I mentioned that we want to compare students to other students within the same school year, meaning that at some point, we're going to have to equate **SchoolYear** from the outer instance of *dbo.ExamGrades* to **SchoolYear** from the instance inside the subquery. Without the ability to alias tables, how would we equate the two; WHERE SchoolYear = SchoolYear? It's not clear which table is being referred to with each invocation of **SchoolYear**; they are ambiguous.

However, this problem can be alleviated by prefacing each column with the alias of the table it's coming from. The column b.SchoolYear is coming from the instance of *dbo.ExamGrades* inside the subquery, because that table is aliased as b.

I made a point in chapter 6.1 that you cannot refer to aliases in a WHERE clause since they have not been applied yet, but it would appear as though this rule has been broken in Query 6-8; I'm referring to aliases in the same query in which I applied them. There is an exception to this rule. Since tables are the first thing to be processed by the query engine, their aliases are applied early, meaning that you *can* refer to table aliases throughout a query.

Let's run through this query step-by-step.

1. The query will begin with the first row (Gina Melvin) from *dbo.ExamGrades* on the fourth line. This will be the "outer" table, and is aliased as a.
2. SQL will begin to evaluate the outer WHERE clause. The WHERE clause will be true if the value of **Grade** for that particular row (76) is greater than the value generated by the subquery.
3. The subquery draws from a new copy of the same table, *dbo.ExamGrades*, but is aliased as b. The WHERE clause in the subquery states that it will only retain the rows where b.SchoolYear = a.SchoolYear. Since the outer table is aliased as a, the value of a.SchoolYear is "Freshman." Therefore, the subquery will only keep the rows of the freshman students.
4. The subquery calculates the average grade of the freshmen students.
5. The value for **Grade** from the outer query can be compared against this average value to determine whether or not to keep the row in the results.

Once SQL progresses to the next row, **SchoolYear** changes to "Junior." The process will repeat again, except this time, the subquery will calculate the average for all of the students who are juniors. The results of Query 6-8 are shown in Table 6-6.

Query Results		
Student	**Grade**	**SchoolYear**
Gina Melvin	76	Freshman
Robert Harris	84	Freshman
Donny Wilmoth	76	Junior
John Fleck	77	Senior
Clayton Wheeler	88	Sophomore
Barbara Fisher	99	Sophomore

Table 6-6

This goes back to the definition that was presented in the beginning of this chapter. This particular example was a *correlated* subquery, because the average values that the subquery was calculating were being determined by the school year passed to it from the outer query.

I mentioned earlier that column names repeated throughout both tables need to be aliased to avoid potential problems. But outside of the subquery in Query 6-8, there are no aliases, despite **Student**, **Grade**, and **SchoolYear** being repeated names. This is because the outer query cannot see what's happening inside the subquery; it lives in its own little world, and has no idea what the alias of b is. Therefore, we can select from the outer *dbo.ExamGrades* table as if the inner one never existed. The subquery, however, *can* see everything that's going on above it, and must keep track of similarly-named columns by aliasing them in order to avoid confusion.

6.4 Checking if a Particular Row Exists

It is sometimes desirable to know that a row exists within a dataset, regardless of what actual data is contained within that row. Consider the following scenario, a teacher has given two exams in his class. After the first exam, several students dropped the class, and did not take the second exam. The teacher suspects that if a student did well on the first exam, then that student probably did not drop the class, and stayed to take the second exam. Therefore, he wants to get all of the *first* exam grades of students who have also taken the second exam. The following two tables are the grades for the two tests.

dbo.ExamGrades1		dbo.ExamGrades2	
Student	Grade	Student	Grade
Gina Melvin	76	Gina Melvin	79
Donny Wilmoth	76	Donny Wilmoth	80
Jeannie Smith	3	Barbara Fisher	92
Barbara Fisher	99	John Fleck	83
John Fleck	77	Clayton Wheeler	81
Clayton Wheeler	88		
Sarah Rodriguez	7		
Jenna Brenner	54		

Table 6-7 and Table 6-8

Notice that in this scenario, we are checking to see if a particular name merely exists in the second table, we don't actually care about what the second grade was. To accomplish this task, we can use EXISTS.

```
SELECT Columns
  FROM Table
 WHERE EXISTS (Subquery)
```

Syntax 6-2

Referring back to chapter 4.1, a row will be presented in the final result set if the condition(s) given in the WHERE clause are true for that row. An EXISTS clause evaluates to true if the subquery returns any rows.

```
SELECT Student,
       Grade
  FROM dbo.ExamGrades1 AS a
 WHERE EXISTS (SELECT Student
                 FROM dbo.ExamGrades2 AS b
                WHERE b.Student = a.Student)
```

Query 6-9

Query Results	
Student	Grade
Gina Melvin	76
Donny Wilmoth	76
Barbara Fisher	99
John Fleck	77
Clayton Wheeler	88

Table 6-9

Query 6-9 appears quite similar to Query 6-8. In fact, the step-by-step walkthrough is nearly identical as well, but with some minor differences, so let's walk through this one as well:

1. The query will begin with the first row (Gina Melvin) from *dbo.ExamGrades1* on the third line. This will be the "outer" table, and is aliased as a.

2. SQL will begin to evaluate the outer WHERE clause. The WHERE clause will be true if the subquery returns any rows.

3. The subquery draws from the table of grades for the second exam, and is aliased as b. The WHERE clause in the subquery states that it will only retain the rows where b.Student = a.Student. Since the outer table is aliased as a, the value of a.Student is "Gina Melvin." Therefore, the subquery will only keep the rows of students named Gina Melvin.

4. Since Gina Melvin took the second test, she will appear in *dbo.ExamGrades2*, and thus, will appear in the subquery. This causes the entire WHERE clause to evaluate as true for that row, and Gina is displayed in the overall query results. Again, it does not matter what Gina's score was for the second test, it only matters that she *took* the second test.

Once SQL progresses to Jeannie Smith, the subquery will not return any rows, because Jeannie did not take the second exam, and therefore would not appear in *dbo.ExamGrades2*, and by extension, the subquery. The EXISTS clause evaluates as false, meaning that Jeannie's name and first exam grade will not be present in the result set.

We can negate the entire statement by placing the word NOT in front of the EXISTS clause. The negated version of the query would be asking "give me the names and first exam grades of any student whose name does *not* exist in the second exam grades table." By comparison, Jeannie Smith *would* appear in the results of such a query.

6.5   Comparing Against Some, Any, and All Rows

With SQL, it is possible to compare (equals, greater-than, less-than, etc.) a value from one row to multiple values in multiple rows in another table using only one statement (similar to an IN list, but with some added functionality). This is done with the SOME/ANY clause and the ALL clause. One possible implementation of the clauses is shown in Syntax 6-3. The equals sign on line two may be replaced with another operator such as <, >, !=, etc.

```
SELECT Columns,
       CASE WHEN Column = SOME/ANY/ALL (Subquery)
            THEN Some Value
            ELSE Other Value
             END
  FROM Table
```

Syntax 6-3

The easiest way to demonstrate its use is with an example. Consider the following scenario, a teacher has two classes, both of which have taken the same exam. Their grades are listed below.

dbo.ClassGrades_First		dbo.ClassGrades_Second	
Student	**Grade**	**Student**	**Grade**
Bertram Scott	77	Julia Wilkins	62
John Goodyear	63	Wendy Weber	71
Kevin Taylor	84	Jeffrey Nolan	40
Annie Barnes	52	Ervin Whitlock	39
Sam McGinnis	96	Amanda Lansberry	37
Tony Hernandez	72	Glenn Moore	50
Lizzie Johnson	87	Lily Cochrane	74
Marlin Edwards	35	Angelia Johnson	65
Dexter Miller	32	Susanne Dutton	52
Paul McCall	81	Gayle Knight	71

Table 6-10 and Table 6-11

The teacher would like to know which students in the first class have scored higher than *all* of the students in the second class. If they achieved this, we'll display the phrase "Top score" next to their name. If not, we'll display the phrase "Standard score."

This is where the ALL clause is used.

```
SELECT Student,
       Grade,
       CASE WHEN Grade > ALL (SELECT Grade FROM dbo.ClassGrades_Second)
            THEN 'Top score'
            ELSE 'Standard score'
          END AS ScoreType
  FROM dbo.ClassGrades_First
```

Query 6-10

Query Results		
Student	**Grade**	**ScoreType**
Bertram Scott	77	Top score
John Goodyear	63	Standard score
Kevin Taylor	84	Top score
Annie Barnes	52	Standard score
Sam McGinnis	96	Top score
Tony Hernandez	72	Standard score
Lizzie Johnson	87	Top score
Marlin Edwards	35	Standard score
Dexter Miller	32	Standard score
Paul McCall	81	Top score

Table 6-12

Note that the subquery inside the ALL clause must only return a single column. Since the maximum score in the second class was a 74, anyone in the first class who scored a 75 or above will be designated as someone with a top score.

We can take it one step further by breaking down the "standard score" logic. We'll add in criteria that if the student's score in the first class is greater than *any* (but not necessarily all) of the student's scores in the second class, it will display "standard score." But if the student fails to beat any of the scores in the second class, it will display "low score."

To implement being greater than *any* of the scores in the second class, we can use the ANY or SOME clauses. Both are identical and can be used interchangeably.

```
SELECT Student,
       Grade,
       CASE WHEN Grade > ALL (SELECT Grade FROM dbo.ClassGrades_Second)
            THEN 'Top score'
            WHEN Grade > ANY (SELECT Grade FROM dbo.ClassGrades_Second)
            THEN 'Standard score'
            ELSE 'Low score'
          END AS ScoreType
  FROM dbo.ClassGrades_First
```

Query 6-11

Let's run through this query step-by-step.

1. The query will begin with the first row (Bertram Scott) from *dbo.ClassGrades_First* on the ninth line.
2. SQL will begin to evaluate the CASE statement. The subquery in the first line of the CASE statement generates a list of all grades from the second class, and then SQL checks to see if Bertram's grade is above all of them. He is, so he's designated as a top scorer, and the CASE statement is over for this row.
3. The query will move onto the second row (John Goodyear). The subquery will again generate a list of all grades from the second class, and SQL will compare John's grade against all of them. He beats Julia Wilkin's score of 62, but does not beat Wendy Weber's score of 71, so the ALL branch of the CASE statement is false. At this point, since John did not beat everyone else's score, he cannot be designated as a top scorer. SQL then moves to the next branch, the ANY branch.
4. Once again, the subquery generates a list of grades, and begins comparing John's grade against them. He beats Julia Wilkin's score of 62. He's now beat *at least* one of the grades in the second class, causing the ANY branch of the CASE statement to be true. He is designated as a standard scorer, and the CASE statement is over for this row.
5. Upon reaching Marlin Edwards, he will fail to beat *all* of the grades from the second class, and also fail to beat *any* of the grades from the second class, meaning both the ALL and ANY branches are false. And since none of the branches in the CASE statement were true, he is designated as a low scorer.

The results of Query 6-11 are shown in Table 6-13.

Query Results		
Student	**Grade**	**ScoreType**
Bertram Scott	77	Top score
John Goodyear	63	Standard score
Kevin Taylor	84	Top score
Annie Barnes	52	Standard score
Sam McGinnis	96	Top score
Tony Hernandez	72	Standard score
Lizzie Johnson	87	Top score
Marlin Edwards	35	Low score
Dexter Miller	32	Low score
Paul McCall	81	Top score

Table 6-13

6.6   Selecting Subqueries as a Column

It is possible to select a subquery (both correlated and uncorrelated) as an entirely new column. Consider the earlier scenario where we returned the students whose grade was above the class average. We will modify it a little bit. Instead of filtering out students who are below the class average, we will be listing all students as well as the point difference between the student's score and the class average.

```
SELECT Student,
       Grade,
       Grade - (SELECT AVG(Grade)
                  FROM dbo.ExamGrades) AS DiffAvg
   FROM dbo.ExamGrades
```

Query 6-12

By creating a subquery as before, but instead placing it in the column list like we would any other column, we can generate a new column when the query is run.

Query Results		
Student	Grade	DiffAvg
Gina Melvin	76	10
Donny Wilmoth	76	10
Barbara Fisher	99	33
John Fleck	77	11
Clayton Wheeler	88	22
Robert Harris	84	18
Kenneth Copeland	50	-16
Christine Cox	33	-33
Robert Ruhl	36	-30
Billy Hill	49	-17

Table 6-14

The previous example was an uncorrelated subquery, because the average that was being generated in the subquery wasn't affected by any of the values in the outer query. If we wanted to calculate the difference between the student's grade and the average for their respective school year, we can turn this into a correlated subquery in the same fashion that was described earlier in chapter 6.3; by adding a correlation that **SchoolYear** from the outer query must be equal to **SchoolYear** from the inner query.

6.7 Effects of Subqueries on Performance

A final word of warning: using a subquery can quickly ruin the efficiency of your query. Look at Query 6-12. Every time a new row is read, SQL must (via the subquery) access and scan an entire table, and then compute and return the average grade. This tiny, incremental amount of time it takes to complete this task for each row will be compounded across the entire table. SQL Server may have some optimizations to minimize the impact, but there is no guarantee that it will be very effective.

This is the inherent inefficiency in subqueries; for every row in the main table that you are selecting from, the subquery is executed. One hundred rows means one hundred extra queries. While your results may vary, if you are able to avoid subqueries without too much hassle, it's best to do so.

7 Common Table Expressions

7.1 Single Common Table Expressions

Common table expressions (abbr. CTE), like subqueries, are a way of making temporary tables that contain pre-calculated data in the format of your choosing. CTEs only exist for the duration of the query. Once the query has finished running, the CTE ceases to exist.

```
WITH Alias
  AS (Query)
Main Query
```

Syntax 7-1

Referring back to Query 6-2 and Query 6-3, the problem we ran into when selecting students whose new grade was above a certain threshold, was that we couldn't refer to the aliases of those columns. We were unable to write `WHERE NewGrade...`, and had to instead write `WHERE Grade + 10...`.

From what we've learned in chapter 6, to refer to columns by their aliases, they would need to be placed in a subquery first. In simple scenarios, this method works fine, but as the size and complexity of the query increases (think subqueries within subqueries), it may be beneficial to use CTEs instead. In Query 7-1, I have translated Query 6-4 to function identically, except using a CTE instead of a subquery.

```
WITH NewGradeTable
  AS (SELECT Student,
             Grade + 10 AS NewGrade
        FROM dbo.ExamGrades)
SELECT Student,
       NewGrade
  FROM NewGradeTable
 WHERE NewGrade >= 60
```

Query 7-1

Using this method, the portion of the query that calculates the new column values and applies aliases is separate from the portion that selects the student's information and filters by their grade. At the start of the CTE in Query 7-1, we are saying that the table generated by the query between lines two and four will be given the table alias of *NewGradeTable*. *NewGradeTable* does not have a *dbo* in front because it is not actually a table, it's only a "mask" for a table. When creating a CTE, any derived or calculated columns must be given an alias.

The results of the query inside the CTE aren't actually shown. All that we're doing is telling SQL that if we refer to a table called *NewGradeTable*, we're actually referring to the code, columns, and aliases inside the parentheses. In the main query beginning on line five, we can refer to the alias **NewGrade** instead of `Grade + 10`.

7.2 Multiple Common Table Expressions

We are not limited to only one CTE at a time. Additional CTEs can be added if there are multiple tables involved in a single query, or perhaps multiple operations need to be performed on a single table. This is done simply by adding a comma after the closing parenthesis and placing another **Alias** AS (...) statement.

```
WITH 1st Alias
  AS (1st Query),

    2nd Alias
  AS (2nd Query),
    ...
    Nth Alias
  AS (Nth Query)

Main Query
```

Syntax 7-2

The queries inside the CTEs can refer to any tables in a database. They can even refer to earlier CTEs in the chain. This saves you the effort and confusion of writing multiple nested subqueries. After being calculated, all of the CTEs are available to be used by the main query on the last line. They are *only* visible to the main query. As soon as the main query finishes executing (even if there are more queries after it) the CTEs will no longer be available for use.

CTEs can be placed anywhere in your query; they do *not* need to be written first. If there is any code written before the start of a CTE or chain of CTEs, the last statement before the start of the CTE must terminate with a semicolon.

8 Reading From Multiple Tables

8.1 The Union of Two Tables

It is not always the case that all of the required data is in the same table. For example, there may be one table that contains all customer purchases on one day, and another table (with identical columns) containing all purchases on the following day. If a query needs to make use of all this data at once, the two tables can be temporarily combined by using UNION. If we execute a select statement on two different tables and UNION them together, the results will appear as a single table.

```
SELECT Columns
  FROM 1st Table
 UNION
SELECT Columns
  FROM 2nd Table
```

Syntax 8-1

When doing a UNION, each query should select the same number of columns (the following examples will only use one column for simplicity), and corresponding columns between the tables should be of the same data type. If the first column from the first table has a certain data type, then the first column from the second table should have the same data type, and so on and so forth for additional columns. Each individual query may use WHERE clauses, aliases, subqueries, aggregation, etc. If more than two tables need to be combined, additional UNIONs can be daisy-chained onto the end. Two sample tables are shown below, along with a UNION query that will combine them into a single output.

dbo.UnionTable_1	dbo.UnionTable_2
Student	**Student**
Bertram Scott	Julia Wilkins
John Goodyear	Wendy Weber
Kevin Taylor	Jeffrey Nolan
Annie Barnes	Kevin Taylor

Table 8-1 and Table 8-2

```
SELECT Student
  FROM dbo.UnionTable_1
 UNION
SELECT Student
  FROM dbo.UnionTable_2
```

Query 8-1

Query Results
Student
Bertram Scott
John Goodyear
Kevin Taylor
Annie Barnes
Julia Wilkins
Wendy Weber
Jeffrey Nolan

Table 8-3

Notice that Kevin Taylor appears in both tables, but only appears once in the results of the query. If the same row appears in both tables, then a UNION will *not* show two copies of the row. It will instead only show a single row. If the repeated rows *must* be shown, the UNION should be changed to a UNION ALL.

```
SELECT Columns
   FROM 1st Table
 UNION ALL
SELECT Columns
   FROM 2nd Table
```

Syntax 8-2

Changing line three of Query 8-1 to read UNION ALL will cause Kevin Taylor to appear twice in the results.

Query Results
Student
Bertram Scott
John Goodyear
Kevin Taylor
Annie Barnes
Julia Wilkins
Wendy Weber
Jeffrey Nolan
Kevin Taylor

Table 8-4

When using UNION with multiple columns, the *entire row* from the first table must match to the *entire row* from the second table in order for the duplicate copy to be removed. If even one column in either of the rows is different, both copies will be shown. Partial unions cannot be made, i.e., you cannot exclude a row from the second table just because *some* of the values matched to a row in the first table. Every value must match.

8.2 The Difference Between Two Tables

Using EXCEPT in SQL will find the difference between two tables by looking for the rows that appear in the first table but not the second table.

```
SELECT Columns
  FROM 1st Table
EXCEPT
SELECT Columns
  FROM 2nd Table
```

Syntax 8-3

EXCEPT has the same limitations as UNION and UNION ALL; both queries should select the same number of columns, and the corresponding columns in both tables should be of the same general data type in order for it to function properly.

Picture the following scenario: a local college offers calculus classes at two different levels, introductory, and advanced. Students must take the introductory class before they can move on to the advanced course. The head of the mathematics department wants to know which students took the introductory class but did *not* progress to the advanced class.

You have two tables of student names. The first has the names of all students who were enrolled in the introductory class in the previous semester. The second table has the names of all students who are enrolled in the advanced class *this* semester.

dbo.IntroCalculus	dbo.AdvancedCalculus
Student	**Student**
Carole Costigan	Carole Costigan
Robert Hurst	Brian Lee
Brian Lee	Mary Perez
David Mann	Delia Lucas
Olivia Failla	Alex Jimenez
Crystal Sabia	
Mary Perez	
Delia Lucas	
Eric Saucier	
Alex Jimenez	

Table 8-5 and Table 8-6

To find the difference between these two tables, EXCEPT must be used.

```
SELECT Student
  FROM dbo.IntroCalculus
EXCEPT
SELECT Student
  FROM dbo.AdvancedCalculus
```

Query 8-2

Query Results
Student
Crystal Sabia
David Mann
Eric Saucier
Olivia Failla
Robert Hurst

Table 8-7

The query is saying "give me the names of the students who took the introductory class *except* for those who are also in the advanced class." Since these five students were enrolled in the beginner class, but not the advanced class, they are the ones who appear in the query results.

When using EXCEPT with multiple columns, the *entire row* from the first table must match to the *entire row* from the second table in order for it to be excluded. If even one column in either of the rows is different, the exclusion will not take place. Partial exceptions cannot be made, i.e., you cannot exclude a row from the first table just because *some* of the values matched to a row in the second table. Every value must match.

8.3 The Similarities Between Two Tables

EXCEPT works to find the difference between two tables. The reverse of this would be to find the similarities between two tables. This is where INTERSECT is used.

```
    SELECT Columns
      FROM 1st Table
INTERSECT
    SELECT Columns
      FROM 2nd Table
```

Syntax 8-4

Again, the same limitations apply to INTERSECT as to EXCEPT and UNION/UNION ALL. Going back to the calculus class example, to find the students who have taken *both* beginner calculus and advanced calculus, the query would be the following:

```
    SELECT Student
      FROM dbo.IntroCalculus
INTERSECT
    SELECT Student
      FROM dbo.AdvancedCalculus
```

Query 8-3

Query Results
Student
Alex Jimenez
Brian Lee
Carole Costigan
Delia Lucas
Mary Perez

Table 8-8

Since these five students were enrolled in both the beginner class *and* the advanced class, they are the ones who appear in the query results.

When using INTERSECT with multiple columns, the *entire row* from the first table must match to the *entire row* from the second table in order for the duplicate copy to be shown. If even one column in either of the rows is different, neither copy will be shown. Partial intersections cannot be made, i.e., you cannot include a row from the first table just because *some* of the values matched to a row in the second table. Every value must match.

8.4 Joining Tables Together

Joins are SQL's way of relating two or more tables so that users can retrieve data from any of them in the same query. Unlike a UNION, these tables can be entirely different, and contain different columns. Consider the following table, which shows a few purchases made by customers at an online store.

dbo.Purchases							
PurchaseNumber	PurchasePrice	PurchaseDate	Name	Address	City	US_State	Zip
6921	9.85	2020-05-13	Jay Edwards	212 Clinton Rd	Havelock	NC	28532
1311	52.05	2020-05-01	Emery Pawlak	3276 Glendale St	Desert Haven	TX	79837
3805	1.12	2020-07-12	Margaret Briggs	3638 Reeves St	Foretsville	WI	54213
8088	99.27	2020-08-06	Adam Goins	94 Goff Ave	Martin	MI	49070

Table 8-9

There is nothing special here, but it is not always the case that the information about the purchases will be in the same table as the information about the addresses. Quite often you'll see something like the following.

dbo.Purchases			
PurchaseNumber	PurchasePrice	PurchaseDate	FKey_Address
6921	9.85	2020-05-13	1
1311	52.05	2020-05-01	2
3805	1.12	2020-07-12	3
8088	99.27	2020-08-06	4

Table 8-10

dbo.Addresses					
PKey_Address	Name	Address	City	US_State	Zip
1	Jay Edwards	212 Clinton Rd	Havelock	NC	28532
2	Emery Pawlak	3276 Glendale St	Desert Haven	TX	79837
3	Margaret Briggs	3638 Reeves St	Foretsville	WI	54213
4	Adam Goins	94 Goff Ave	Martin	MI	49070

Table 8-11

Why would anyone want to have their data structured like this? It offers no apparent improvement over the previous single table. In fact, it's actually worse. It's two tables instead of one, and new data has been introduced by way of the **FKey_Address**, and **PKey_Address** columns. But we'll see in just a moment that splitting the data into two tables serves an incredibly useful purpose. First thing's first though, what are these "key" columns, and what do they do?

Keys are the actual column by which two tables are correlated. If you want to reunite this data side-by-side again, you'll have to connect the two tables together via the key column(s). Think of it like a coat check at a restaurant. You and your coat are separated. The clerk puts a tag on your coat with a number, and you are given a tag with the same number. Later, when you need to pick up your coat, you give the clerk your tag, and he or she matches the number on the tag to the number on the coat, at which point you and your coat are reunited.

In the case of our sample tables, they are related to each other through the *foreign* and *primary* address keys, **FKey_Address**, and **PKey_Address** (we'll learn more about what constitutes a primary and foreign key in just a bit). Look at purchase number 6921 in Table 8-10. If we want to figure out which address this order was sent to, we'll have to see what address key is on this order, which is one, and look up that key in Table 8-11. We find that it was shipped to Jay Edwards in Havelock, NC.

But that still doesn't explain why it's better to structure your data such that you require joins. For that, we'll take a quick detour, and use the following table for our examples.

dbo.Purchases							
PurchaseNumber	PurchasePrice	PurchaseDate	Name	Address	City	US_State	Zip
1	43.78	2020-07-02	John Smith	18 Front St	Joilet	IL	60435
2	18.24	2020-08-28	John Smith	18 Front St	Joilet	IL	60435
3	84.64	2020-09-15	John Smith	18 Front St	Joilet	IL	60435

Table 8-12

What about this table do you think can be improved? There is a significant amount of redundancy in the name and address columns (**Name**, **Address**, **City**, **US_State**, and **Zip**). Every time the customer makes an order, these fields are repeated. It takes up unnecessary space, and in the event that his address needs to be updated, SQL will need to update as many rows as there are purchases for him.

We'll give Table 8-12 the same treatment, and split up the purchases from the addresses.

dbo.Purchases					dbo.Addresses					
PurchaseNumber	PurchasePrice	PurchaseDate	Key		Key	Name	Address	City	US_State	Zip
1	43.78	2020-07-02	1		1	John Smith	18 Front St	Joilet	IL	60435
2	18.24	2020-08-28	1							
3	84.64	2020-09-15	1							

Table 8-13 and Table 8-14

You'll probably immediately recognize the lack of symmetry; three orders and only one address. But again, this is what we want. John Smith's purchase on July 2nd was split up into its constituents. The address information was inserted into *dbo.Addresses*, and was given a key of one. The same key, along with the purchase information, was inserted into *dbo.Purchases*. If someone wished to know where the first order was shipped to, they would need to look up the address whose key is one.

The second purchase was then split up into its constituents, but the address was not inserted into the address table. We had already inserted that same address earlier, so instead of inserting the same address again, we can simply reuse the key, meaning only the purchase information for this row is inserted, along with a key of one. It may be clearer now why this structure is beneficial. A customer may have 1,000 purchases which were all shipped to the same address, but thanks to this data structure, we no longer have to repeat the address data, saving us on space and the amount of overhead needed to run a query. As long as all of those purchases have valid address keys, we can figure out where any of the orders was shipped to.

If an order is placed that uses a different address, this new address would be inserted into *dbo.Addresses* with a key of two. Because of this, no key can ever be reused in *dbo.Addresses*, and each key corresponds to a unique address.

8.4.1 Composing a Join statement

Now that we know what joins are, and the "why" behind joins, we need to know the "how." More specifically, how we (temporarily) reunite the purchases and addresses and display them as they originally were in Table 8-9. We will have to take *dbo.Purchases* (Table 8-10), and JOIN *dbo.Addresses* (Table 8-11) to it. The syntax of a JOIN is shown in Syntax 8-5.

```
   SELECT Columns
     FROM Fact Table
Type JOIN Dimension Table
       ON Foreign Key = Primary Key
```

Syntax 8-5

A JOIN typically requires at least six fields supplied from the user: the two tables that are being joined, the columns that will be selected from both tables, the type of JOIN that will be performed, and the keys that will relate the two tables (a.k.a. the join criteria).

To recreate Table 8-9, we will need **PurchaseNumber**, **PurchasePrice**, and **PurchaseDate** from *dbo.Purchases*, and **Name**, **Address**, **City**, **US_State**, and **Zip** from *dbo.Addresses*. Outside of building the query, the keys don't contain any useful information, so they will be omitted from the columns that are selected.

```
   SELECT PurchaseNumber,
          PurchasePrice,
          PurchaseDate,
          Name,
          Address,
          City,
          US_State,
          Zip
     FROM Fact Table
Type JOIN Dimension Table
       ON Foreign Key = Primary Key
```

Query 8-4

The *fact table* is typically the one that contains unique information (in this case, the purchases), and references another table in order to access repeating data (the addresses). The *dimension table* is the one that is *being referenced* in order to get that repeating data. Therefore, *dbo.Purchases* is the fact table, and *dbo.Addresses* is the dimension table.

```
    SELECT PurchaseNumber,
           PurchasePrice,
           PurchaseDate,
           Name,
           Address,
           City,
           US_State,
           Zip
      FROM dbo.Purchases
Type JOIN dbo.Addresses
        ON Foreign Key = Primary Key
```

Query 8-5

As a general rule, the fact table contains the foreign key, and the dimension table contains the primary key. Larger and more complicated data structures may eschew this rule and have tables with both primary *and* foreign keys.

Moving on, we can relate a purchase with an address by equating the primary and foreign key columns from both tables.

```
    SELECT PurchaseNumber,
           PurchasePrice,
           PurchaseDate,
           Name,
           Address,
           City,
           US_State,
           Zip
      FROM dbo.Purchases
Type JOIN dbo.Addresses
        ON FKey_Address = PKey_Address
```

Query 8-6

All that remains to be entered is the type of JOIN, at which point the query will be fully constructed and can be executed.

Before moving on, one thing to note, you are not limited to only one join criteria. In this example, there is only one relationship necessary to connect a purchase with an address (FKey_Address = PKey_Address). Depending on the structures of the tables, it may be necessary to equate multiple columns in order to produce the desired result. This will be explored further shortly. Likewise, it is possible to use other operators (greater-than, greater-than-or-equal-to, less-than, etc.) in the join criteria.

If you are joining any additional tables, you can place more JOINs in series. Each must have their own equating of a primary and foreign key as well. Any WHERE, GROUP BY, etc. clauses should be placed after all of the joins.

8.4.2 Types of Joins

There are four main types of joins in SQL, LEFT, RIGHT, INNER, and FULL OUTER[8]. Each one functions slightly differently, and the appropriate type to use will depend on the needs of the user. There will be a slight change to both the purchases and addresses table.

dbo.Purchases			
PurchaseNumber	**PurchasePrice**	**PurchaseDate**	**FKey_Address**
6921	9.85	2020-05-13	1
1311	52.05	2020-05-01	2
3805	1.12	2020-07-12	3
8088	99.27	2020-08-06	4
7402	13.15	2020-06-05	5

Table 8-15

dbo.Addresses					
PKey_Address	**Name**	**Address**	**City**	**US_State**	**Zip**
1	Jay Edwards	212 Clinton Rd	Havelock	NC	28532
2	Emery Pawlak	3276 Glendale St	Desert Haven	TX	79837
3	Margaret Briggs	3638 Reeves St	Foretsville	WI	54213
4	Adam Goins	94 Goff Ave	Martin	MI	49070
6	Devin Bellew	980 Kelley Rd	Gulfport	MS	39501

Table 8-16

Notice that there is a foreign key in *dbo.Purchases* that does not exist in the primary keys of *dbo.Addresses*, and there is a primary key in *dbo.Addresses* that does not exist in foreign keys of *dbo.Purchases*. This is important when describing the functionality of joins.

Using a LEFT JOIN in Query 8-6 will return all of the rows from the first listed table, *dbo.Purchases*. If a key match to the second table, *dbo.Addresses*, is found for a particular row, we will have access to the address information for that purchase. Even if no match is found, the purchase row will be displayed in the results, but all of the address information will be null.

Query Results							
PurchaseNumber	**PurchasePrice**	**PurchaseDate**	**Name**	**Address**	**City**	**US_State**	**Zip**
6921	9.85	2020-05-13	Jay Edwards	212 Clinton Rd	Havelock	NC	28532
1311	52.05	2020-05-01	Emery Pawlak	3276 Glendale St	Desert Haven	TX	79837
3805	1.12	2020-07-12	Margaret Briggs	3638 Reeves St	Foretsville	WI	54213
8088	99.27	2020-08-06	Adam Goins	94 Goff Ave	Martin	MI	49070
7402	13.15	2020-06-05	NULL	NULL	NULL	NULL	NULL

Table 8-17

All five customers from *dbo.Purchases* are displayed in the results. The only purchase without address information is number 7402. Its foreign key of five did not find a match in the primary keys of *dbo.Addresses*, but it is displayed, nonetheless.

---

[8] There is a fifth, lesser-used type known as a CROSS join. It will be discussed briefly later in chapter 8.4.4.

An INNER JOIN will only return the rows from the first table where there is a key match to the second table. Because of this, we are guaranteed to have valid address information for these rows.

Query Results							
PurchaseNumber	PurchasePrice	PurchaseDate	Name	Address	City	US_State	Zip
6921	9.85	2020-05-13	Jay Edwards	212 Clinton Rd	Havelock	NC	28532
1311	52.05	2020-05-01	Emery Pawlak	3276 Glendale St	Desert Haven	TX	79837
3805	1.12	2020-07-12	Margaret Briggs	3638 Reeves St	Foretsville	WI	54213
8088	99.27	2020-08-06	Adam Goins	94 Goff Ave	Martin	MI	49070

Table 8-18

Only four of the five customers from *dbo.Purchases* are displayed in the results. Since purchase number 7402 was unable to find a match to its key, it was excluded from the result set.

A RIGHT JOIN is the same as a LEFT JOIN, except in reverse. It will return all of the rows from the second table, *dbo.Addresses*. If a match to *dbo.Purchases* is found on the key for a particular row, we will have access to the purchase information for that row. Even if no key match is found, the row will be displayed in the results, but all of the purchase information will be null.

Query Results							
PurchaseNumber	PurchasePrice	PurchaseDate	Name	Address	City	US_State	Zip
6921	9.85	2020-05-13	Jay Edwards	212 Clinton Rd	Havelock	NC	28532
1311	52.05	2020-05-01	Emery Pawlak	3276 Glendale St	Desert Haven	TX	79837
3805	1.12	2020-07-12	Margaret Briggs	3638 Reeves St	Foretsville	WI	54213
8088	99.27	2020-08-06	Adam Goins	94 Goff Ave	Martin	MI	49070
NULL	NULL	NULL	Devin Bellew	980 Kelley Rd	Gulfport	MS	39501

Table 8-19

All five addresses from *dbo.Addresses* are displayed in the results. The only address without a purchase is Devin Bellew at 980 Kelley Rd. His primary key of six did not find a match in the foreign keys of *dbo.Purchases*, but it is displayed, nonetheless.

A FULL OUTER JOIN will include all rows from the first table, and all rows from the second table, regardless of if a match on the key is found.

Query Results							
PurchaseNumber	PurchasePrice	PurchaseDate	Name	Address	City	US_State	Zip
6921	9.85	2020-05-13	Jay Edwards	212 Clinton Rd	Havelock	NC	28532
1311	52.05	2020-05-01	Emery Pawlak	3276 Glendale St	Desert Haven	TX	79837
3805	1.12	2020-07-12	Margaret Briggs	3638 Reeves St	Foretsville	WI	54213
8088	99.27	2020-08-06	Adam Goins	94 Goff Ave	Martin	MI	49070
7402	13.15	2020-06-05	NULL	NULL	NULL	NULL	NULL
NULL	NULL	NULL	Devin Bellew	980 Kelley Rd	Gulfport	MS	39501

Table 8-20

This table is a composite of the LEFT JOIN and RIGHT JOIN query results. The purchases with a key match to the addresses table are present. Purchase number 7402, for which there was no address, and Devin Bellew, a customer for whom there was no purchase, are both present.

8.4.3 Intended Duplicates in Joins

The sample tables in chapter 8.4.2 show a one-to-one relationship. Aside from the two unmatched entries that I purposely placed there, each row in the fact table joined to exactly one row in the dimension table. However, this isn't always the case. In fact, it's probably rarely ever the case. Most likely, you'll have a many-to-one, or one-to-many relationship between tables. This means that a row from one table will join to multiple rows in the second table or vice versa.

Look back at Table 8-13 (*dbo.Purchases*). It has three rows for purchases, but *dbo.Addresses* only has one row. If your join criteria was that **Key** from *dbo.Purchases* equals **Key** from *dbo.Addresses*, then technically every row from *dbo.Purchases* should match to the one row from *dbo.Addresses*. The one address will be duplicated three times in the results, once for each purchase, and the resultant table will appear like Table 8-12 (which was our original goal). This is precisely the point of structuring data in a many-to-one/one-to-many fashion; we can save space in a table/database, yet still return to the form of the original table by carefully leveraging the creation of duplicates.

This method is not without its drawbacks, however. If you aren't careful with crafting your join statements, you run the risk of creating duplicates where there shouldn't be.

8.4.4   Unintended Duplicates in Joins

Recall from before that each key in *dbo.Addresses* was unique within the entire table. Now imagine the rules are switched such that keys may repeat as long as they are in different states, e.g., New York, Pennsylvania, and Connecticut may all have their own respective addresses with a key of one, but no state by itself can have more than one addresses with the same key.

This means that a purchase can no longer be linked to an address by looking up *just* the address key. It would be necessary to know both the key *and* the state. Observe the following two tables. I've only selected John Smith's first purchase from Table 8-12, but I've also added a new customer from a different state, along with their purchase and their address. The address table now has two rows with key values of one (since we've established that keys can repeat, as long as they are in different states).

dbo.Purchases			
PurchaseNumber	PurchasePrice	PurchaseDate	FKey_Address
1	43.78	2020-07-02	1
2	32.91	2020-07-23	1

Table 8-21

dbo.Addresses					
PKey_Address	Name	Address	City	US_State	Zip
1	John Smith	18 Front St	Joilet	IL	60435
1	Jane Doe	54 Post Rd	Windsor	CT	06905

Table 8-22

What will happen if we run Query 8-6 (as a `LEFT JOIN`) with no modifications? SQL will look up the address key for purchase number one in *dbo.Addresses* and find multiple matching rows. Since both the 18 Front St. address *and* the 54 Post Rd. address have a key of one, both combinations of purchase number one belonging to John Smith and purchase number one belonging to Jane Doe will be included in the results. Likewise, the same thing will occur with purchase number two. This is referred to as the *Cartesian product* of the two tables.

Query Results							
PurchaseNumber	PurchasePrice	PurchaseDate	Name	Address	City	US_State	Zip
1	43.78	2020-07-02	John Smith	18 Front St	Joilet	IL	60435
1	43.78	2020-07-02	Jane Doe	54 Post Rd	Windsor	CT	06905
2	32.91	2020-07-23	John Smith	18 Front St	Joilet	IL	60435
2	32.91	2020-07-23	Jane Doe	54 Post Rd	Windsor	CT	06905

Table 8-23

This goes back to what I mentioned earlier about unintended duplicates, and the possibility of needing to equate multiple columns in a `JOIN` order to produce the desired result. To solve this problem, *dbo.Purchases* would require some way of connecting to *dbo.Addresses* based on state. Perhaps *dbo.Purchases* was originally created with a column **FKey_State**, and *dbo.Addresses* was created with **PKey_State**.

dbo.Purchases				
PurchaseNumber	PurchasePrice	PurchaseDate	FKey_Address	FKey_State
1	43.78	2020-07-02	1	1
2	32.91	2020-07-23	1	2

Table 8-24

dbo.Addresses						
PKey_Address	PKey_State	Name	Address	City	US_State	Zip
1	1	John Smith	18 Front St	Joilet	IL	60435
1	2	Jane Doe	54 Post Rd	Windsor	CT	06905

Table 8-25

With this new layout, both the address and state keys can be equated in the JOIN to ensure no duplicates are formed.

```
   SELECT PurchaseNumber,
          PurchasePrice,
          PurchaseDate,
          Name,
          Address,
          City,
          US_State,
          Zip
     FROM dbo.Purchases
LEFT JOIN dbo.Addresses
       ON FKey_Address = PKey_Address
      AND FKey_State = PKey_State
```

Query 8-7

Query Results							
PurchaseNumber	PurchasePrice	PurchaseDate	Name	Address	City	US_State	Zip
1	43.78	2020-07-02	John Smith	18 Front St	Joilet	IL	60435
2	32.91	2020-07-23	Jane Doe	54 Post Rd	Windsor	CT	06905

Table 8-26

Query 8-6, unmodified, was insufficient to generate the desired results, as the join criteria was too loose. The additional criteria given in Query 8-7 tightened up the requirements to have a valid join, and thus produced the correct result.

Before moving on, if you *do* desire the cartesian product of two tables, you can use a CROSS join. Each combination of rows from the first table and rows from the second table will be displayed, similar to Table 8-23. This particular type of join does *not* use join criteria.

8.4.5 Aliasing in Join Statements

Like we saw in chapter 6.3, when querying against multiple tables with similar (or identical) column names, care must be taken to avoid ambiguity. It may be necessary to alias the tables and prefix the columns with the alias of its respective table. The same is true with joins. In the previous examples, the names of the tables and the names of their respective columns were all unique, so there was no uncertainty as to which table to draw the information from when running the query, but that is not always the case.

Consider the following example. A company has a promotion where long-time customers will get a refund for a portion of their most recent bill. The table on the left is each customer's most recent bill, and it has two columns, **AccountNumber**, and **TransactionAmount**. The table on the right is the amount that was refunded. It also has two columns, both of which have the same name as their respective column in the first table, **AccountNumber**, and **TransactionAmount**.

dbo.MostRecentBill		dbo.RefundAmount	
AccountNumber	TransactionAmount	AccountNumber	TransactionAmount
84310	15.70	84310	-1.57
81062	5.06	81062	-0.51
75848	29.03	75848	-2.9
43673	29.24	43673	-2.92
88972	53.35	88972	-5.34
86221	32.42	86221	-3.24
40921	85.61	40921	-8.56
20260	52.73	20260	-5.27
80877	50.79	80877	-5.08
65905	63.09	65905	-6.31

Table 8-27 and Table 8-28

A member of the billing team has been asked to compile a report with three columns, the account number, the account's most recent bill amount, and the amount that was refunded for that bill.

Now we must compose the JOIN statement. The two tables are *dbo.MostRecentBill* and *dbo.RefundAmount*. The required columns are the **AccountNumber** from either table, and the **TransactionAmount** from both tables. The two tables will be joined on **AccountNumber**, and a LEFT JOIN will be used (any JOIN type would have worked in this example).

```
   SELECT AccountNumber,
          TransactionAmount,
          TransactionAmount
     FROM dbo.MostRecentBill
LEFT JOIN dbo.RefundAmount
       ON AccountNumber = AccountNumber
```

Query 8-8

The problems are immediately evident. First, the JOIN will fail based on the keys. Both tables have a column named **AccountNumber**. SQL doesn't know if the one to the left of the equals sign refers to *dbo.MostRecentBill* or *dbo.RefundAmount*. The same applies to the one on the right of the equals sign. SQL will stop the execution and throw an ambiguity error.

Second, even if SQL were able to successfully join the two tables, it wouldn't know which columns to select. **TransactionAmount** appears twice because both tables have a column with that name. SQL will again be unsure as to which table is being referred to and will throw an ambiguity error.

There are a few ways to get around this, but ultimately, the easiest way to solve problem is to give both tables an alias. For this example, *dbo.MostRecentBill* will be given an alias of a, and *dbo.RefundAmount* will be given an alias of b.

```
    SELECT a.AccountNumber,
           a.TransactionAmount,
           b.TransactionAmount
      FROM dbo.MostRecentBill AS a
LEFT JOIN dbo.RefundAmount AS b
        ON a.AccountNumber = b.AccountNumber
```

Query 8-9

The aliases are arbitrary and can be chosen at your discretion. In the join criteria, we qualified each **AccountNumber** with either an a. or a b. to signify which table they are coming from. The same was done to the selected columns.

Query Results		
AccountNumber	**TransactionAmount**	**TransactionAmount**
84310	15.70	-1.57
81062	5.06	-0.51
75848	29.03	-2.9
43673	29.24	-2.92
88972	53.35	-5.34
86221	32.42	-3.24
40921	85.61	-8.56
20260	52.73	-5.27
80877	50.79	-5.08
65905	63.09	-6.31

Table 8-29

Before moving on, I want to discuss the use of the asterisk (selecting all columns) in joins. If you have two tables joined together, and use SELECT *, your result set will be all columns from all of the tables. The * can be aliased so that you may select all of the columns from only one of the tables, and manually list the rest.

Assuming you are joining two tables, a and b, the phrase SELECT * is equivalent to SELECT a.*, b.*. This is a shorthand way of saying "select all columns from table a, and then all columns from table b." To select *all* columns from table a, and only *some* of the columns from table b, the query would begin with SELECT a.*, b.**Columns**.

8.4.6 Venn Diagram View of Joins

No chapter on joins would be complete without the Venn diagram portion. This is a handy way to visualize what information will be selected with each type of `JOIN`. Each circle represents a table, and the intersection of the two circles represents the data where a key match was found.

LEFT JOIN

Figure 8-1

RIGHT JOIN

Figure 8-2

INNER JOIN

Figure 8-3

FULL OUTER JOIN

Figure 8-4

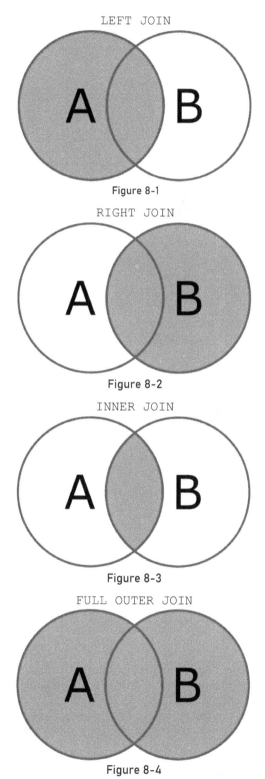

LEFT anti-JOIN[9]

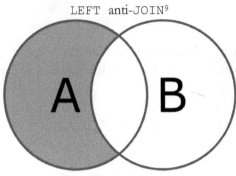

Figure 8-5

RIGHT anti-JOIN[10]

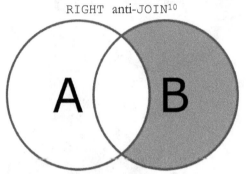

Figure 8-6

FULL OUTER anti-JOIN[11]

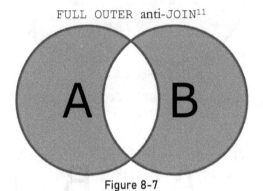

Figure 8-7

---

[9] A LEFT anti-JOIN is written the same way as a regular LEFT JOIN, except it also uses the condition WHERE **B.Key** IS NULL. This will return rows from table *A* which have no key match to table *B* (the key values are exclusive to table *A*).

[10] A RIGHT anti-JOIN is written the same way as a regular RIGHT JOIN, except it also uses the condition WHERE **A.Key** IS NULL. This will return rows from table *B* which have no key match to table *A* (the key values are exclusive to table *B*).

[11] A FULL OUTER anti-JOIN is written the way same as a regular FULL OUTER JOIN, except it also uses the condition WHERE **A.Key** IS NULL OR **B.Key** IS NULL. This will return rows from both table *A* and table *B* which have no key matches to each other. Essentially, it is a FULL OUTER JOIN minus an INNER JOIN (the key values are exclusive to either table *A* or table *B*).

8.5 Joining to a Subquery (a.k.a. Apply)

The easiest way to describe an OUTER APPLY is that it is half a subquery, and half a JOIN. Going back to chapter 6.6, we can place an entire subquery in the column list as though it were its own column. Consider the following scenario. As the teacher of a class, you wish to generate a table containing your student's names and grades from *dbo.ExamGrades*, as well as the difference between their grade and the class average, and the difference between their grade and the class high score.

It is possible to complete this task using the same query that was described in the subqueries chapter, modified to include the max grade as well.

```
SELECT Student,
       Grade,
       Grade - (SELECT AVG(Grade) FROM dbo.ExamGrades) AS DiffAvg,
       Grade - (SELECT MAX(Grade) FROM dbo.ExamGrades) AS DiffMax
  FROM dbo.ExamGrades
```

Query 8-10

Query Results			
Student	**Grade**	**DiffAvg**	**DiffMax**
Gina Melvin	76	10	-23
Donny Wilmoth	76	10	-23
Barbara Fisher	99	33	0
John Fleck	77	11	-22
Clayton Wheeler	88	22	-11
Robert Harris	84	18	-15
Kenneth Copeland	50	-16	-49
Christine Cox	33	-33	-66
Robert Ruhl	36	-30	-63
Billy Hill	49	-17	-50

Table 8-30

But this method is not without its problems. The first is that the same table is being referenced twice for information that could theoretically be returned in one scan of the table (AVG and MAX). The second is that if a change in logic is needed in the subquery, it would be necessary to make as many changes as there are subqueries. If there are ten subqueries, then the table is being scanned ten times. If a change is required, then all ten subqueries need to be changed.

This is where the OUTER APPLY becomes useful. Up to now, subqueries have only allowed us to return one column or value at a time. The crux of an OUTER APPLY is that it operates as a subquery (it executes a query for every row in the main table), but like a JOIN, it gives access to multiple columns at a time instead of just one.

```
     SELECT Columns
       FROM Table
OUTER APPLY (SELECT Columns
              FROM Table) AS Alias
```

Syntax 8-6

An alias for the entire subquery inside the parentheses is required. Like subqueries, aliasing the tables and columns may be necessary if you are creating a correlated subquery or if column names repeat throughout both tables. When in doubt, add an alias.

```
    SELECT a.Student,
           a.Grade,
           a.Grade - b.AvgGrade AS DiffAvg,
           a.Grade - b.MaxGrade AS DiffMax
      FROM dbo.ExamGrades AS a
OUTER APPLY (SELECT AVG(Grade) AS AvgGrade,
                   MAX(Grade) AS MaxGrade
              FROM dbo.ExamGrades) AS b
```

Query 8-11

With this method, we can calculate both the average grade and the max grade using one subquery (the OUTER APPLY), instead of querying the table twice. The results of Query 8-11 will be identical to Table 8-30.

Query 8-11 is an example of an uncorrelated subquery. If we were to modify the query to only compare against students in the same grade (like Query 6-8, a *correlated* subquery), we would need to alias the table inside the subquery, and add a filter equating the school years from both tables.

There is another advantage to using OUTER APPLY when the situation arises; the ability to select which records—and the number of records—that the subquery will return. Normally in a JOIN, if one row in the fact table matches up to three rows in the dimension table (based on the join criteria), you will get three rows returned to you (as shown in chapter 8.4.3). With an OUTER APPLY, as well as subqueries in general, you can specify that you only want, perhaps, *one* row returned to you, even if there are three matches. And on top of that, you can order the rows, so you can select exactly which one row you want.

Observe the following two tables. The first, *dbo.Customers*, contains the account numbers of customers at an online retailer. The second, *dbo.Purchases*, contains some of their purchases. Our goal will be to find the maximum value of **PurchasePrice** for each customer (this can be achieved using aggregate functions, but we'll complete this example using OUTER APPLY).

dbo.Customers	
AccountNumber	CustomerName
821050	Annie Robinson
656972	Bruce Foster

Table 8-31

dbo.Purchases	
AccountNumber	PurchasePrice
821050	24.11
656972	74.90
656972	9.14
821050	56.78

Table 8-32

104

If we attempt to use a JOIN, our results would just be the Cartesian product (four rows—two purchases for each of two customers) of these two tables; not what we want. We are expecting only one row per customer. We could use an OUTER APPLY as shown in Query 8-12, but that would also not solve our problem, as the results would be identical to a JOIN[12].

```
SELECT  a.AccountNumber,
        a.CustomerName,
        b.PurchasePrice
  FROM dbo.Customers AS a
        OUTER APPLY (SELECT AccountNumber,
                            PurchasePrice
                       FROM dbo.Purchases AS p
                      WHERE a.AccountNumber = p.AccountNumber) AS b
```

Query 8-12

Another possibility is to add a stipulation to the OUTER APPLY in Query 8-12 to select only the TOP 1 purchase for each customer (meaning that we won't get a Cartesian product). We'll indeed return only one row per customer, but there's no guarantee that the row will correspond to the customer's highest value for **PurchasePrice** (Table 8-33).

	Query Results	
AccountNumber	**CustomerName**	**PurchasePrice**
821050	Annie Robinson	24.11
656972	Bruce Foster	74.90

Table 8-33

The top one row will be whichever record happens to come first in the table for that customer, regardless of how much the price was. In Table 8-33, Bruce Foster's row corresponds to his most costly purchase, $74.90, but this is purely coincidence. Annie Robinson's row will correspond to her $24.11 purchase, *not* her $56.78 purchase. The solution to these problems is to incorporate both TOP and ORDER BY (as described in chapter 6.2). Since we want the single highest purchase per customer, we will select the top one row, with the data ordered by **PurchasePrice** in descending order. Every row from *dbo.Customers* will kick off the subquery.

```
SELECT  a.AccountNumber,
        a.CustomerName,
        b.PurchasePrice
  FROM dbo.Customers AS a
        OUTER APPLY (  SELECT TOP 1 AccountNumber,
                                    PurchasePrice
                          FROM dbo.Purchases AS p
                         WHERE a.AccountNumber = p.AccountNumber
                      ORDER BY PurchasePrice DESC) AS b
```

Query 8-13

	Query Results	
AccountNumber	**CustomerName**	**PurchasePrice**
821050	Annie Robinson	56.78
656972	Bruce Foster	74.90

Table 8-34

---

[12] Much like a CROSS JOIN, a CROSS APPLY can be used if necessary.

9 Updating and Deleting Data

9.1 Updating Data

9.1.1 Single-Column Updates

The data inside a table are not static. If there is a problem with a column in a particular row, such as a misspelled name, or in many/all rows such as an incorrect calculation, the data may be updated to correct them. Rows are updated using the UPDATE statement. Syntax 9-1 shows the syntax of an UPDATE statement.

```
UPDATE Table
   SET Column = Value
```
Syntax 9-1

The UPDATE statement generally takes three arguments. The first is the table that will be updated. The second is the column within the table that will be updated. The third is the value that the column will be updated to. The third value can be a literal, a calculated value, or even another column, as long as data types aren't mismatched (e.g., setting a string column to be a number or vice versa). If a column must be set to null, you *can* say SET Column = NULL.

Consider Table 9-1, shown below. We're going to ignore **MinimumGrade** for now and focus on just **Grade**.

dbo.ExamGrades		
Student	Grade	MinimumGrade
Melissa Manns	76	70
Douglas Hayes	94	84
Thomas Theodore	88	65

Table 9-1

Suppose each student's grade was calculated incorrectly, and should actually be **Grade** + 5. The proper UPDATE statement for such an adjustment would be:

```
UPDATE dbo.ExamGrades
   SET Grade = Grade + 5
```
Query 9-1

dbo.ExamGrades		
Student	Grade	MinimumGrade
Melissa Manns	81	70
Douglas Hayes	99	84
Thomas Theodore	93	65

Table 9-2

Query 9-1 is a sweeping change; it affects all rows indiscriminately. Updating the column to **Grade** + 5 permanently alters the data. This stands in contrast to earlier when we *selected* **Grade** + 1 in the column list, which was a temporary change.

We don't always want to affect all rows, and would rather target specific rows. The UPDATE statement allows for filtering to certain rows using a WHERE clause. Syntax 9-2 shows the proper use of the UPDATE–WHERE syntax.

```
UPDATE Table
   SET Column = Value
 WHERE Condition
```

Syntax 9-2

Suppose that only Thomas Theodore's grade was incorrect, and required adjustment. To make the same update to Table 9-1, but modified to apply only to Thomas, we would use the UPDATE statement in Query 9-2.

```
UPDATE dbo.ExamGrades
   SET Grade = Grade + 5
 WHERE Student = 'Thomas Theodore'
```

Query 9-2

dbo.ExamGrades		
Student	Grade	MinimumGrade
Melissa Manns	76	70
Douglas Hayes	94	84
Thomas Theodore	93	65

Table 9-3

As a general rule, when writing an UPDATE statement that uses a WHERE clause, I like the name of the table to be the *last* thing I enter into the query. If the query is accidentally executed before the WHERE clause is typed in, the entire table will be updated when only a few rows were originally targeted.

Additionally, UPDATE can be used with TOP to update only the top portion of records by using the following syntax:

```
UPDATE TOP (N) Table
   SET Column = Value
```

Syntax 9-3

Syntax 9-3 can be used with the top P percent of rows as well, not just the top N rows. It must be mentioned that SQL requires the number of percent of rows to be enclosed in parenthesis when used in an UPDATE statement.

Before moving on, I want to give you a quick tip that can save you some typing. In the prior queries, we assigned **Grade** the value of *itself + 5*. A shorter way to write this command is to use an *assignment operator*.

Assignment Operator	Function	Sample Syntax	Equivalent Syntax
+=	Add and assign	SET Grade += 5	SET Grade = Grade + 5
-=	Subtract and assign	SET Grade -= 5	SET Grade = Grade - 5
*=	Multiply and assign	SET Grade *= 5	SET Grade = Grade * 5
/=	Divide and assign	SET Grade /= 5	SET Grade = Grade / 5
%=	Modulo and assign	SET Grade %= 5	SET Grade = Grade % 5

Table 9-4

However, going forward, I will not be using assignment operators, and will instead continue with the syntax I've been using so far.

9.1.2 Multiple-Column Updates

SQL also allows multiple columns to be updated in a single statement. Referring back to Table 9-1 for this example, suppose we want to perform the **Grade** + 5 adjustment, but we also want to decrease **MinimumGrade** by two points.

To do a multiple-column update, we can write more than one *column* = *value* statement, separated by commas.

```
UPDATE Table
   SET 1st Column = Value,
       2nd Column = Value,
       ...
       Nth Column = Value
```

Syntax 9-4

To add five points to **Grade** and subtract two points from **MinimumGrade**, we can use Query 9-3.

```
UPDATE dbo.ExamGrades
   SET Grade = Grade + 5,
       MinimumGrade = MinimumGrade - 2
```

Query 9-3

dbo.ExamGrades		
Student	Grade	MinimumGrade
Melissa Manns	81	68
Douglas Hayes	99	82
Thomas Theodore	93	63

Table 9-5

Adding a WHERE clause is allowed when updating multiple columns, but only one is allowed per UPDATE statement. The following type of query is *not* allowed.

```
UPDATE Table
   SET 1st Column = Value
 WHERE Condition,

   SET 2nd Column = Value
 WHERE Condition,
       ...
   SET Nth Column = Value
 WHERE Condition
```

Syntax 9-5

If there are multiple WHERE clauses, they must be broken up into multiple queries such that each UPDATE statement contains only one WHERE clause.

9.2 Deleting Data

Deleting data in SQL is similar to selecting, updating, and inserting data. There are several different methods that can be used to delete data.

9.2.1 Truncating Tables

The first method of deleting data is the TRUNCATE command. TRUNCATE will completely wipe a table clean; every row will be deleted. Note that the table itself will not be deleted, only the data within.

```
TRUNCATE TABLE Table
```
Syntax 9-6

9.2.2 Deleting Rows

The second method of deleting data is the DELETE command. In its simplest form, the DELETE command can be run as shown in Syntax 9-7.

```
DELETE FROM Table
```
Syntax 9-7

If *table* in Syntax 9-7 were populated with a proper table name and executed, it would function identically to a TRUNCATE command; a blanket delete command where all rows are deleted from the table.

Having two functions which delete all of the data in a table isn't helpful. Fortunately, the DELETE command can be modified to only delete certain rows. Much like how we can add a WHERE clause to an UPDATE statement, we can add a WHERE clause to a DELETE statement so only rows that match certain criteria are removed.

```
DELETE FROM Table
  WHERE Condition
```
Syntax 9-8

If we decided to delete Thomas Theodore from Table 9-5, we would use the following query.

```
DELETE FROM dbo.ExamGrades
  WHERE Student = 'Thomas Theodore'
```
Query 9-4

dbo.ExamGrades		
Student	Grade	MinimumGrade
Melissa Manns	81	68
Douglas Hayes	99	82

Table 9-6

Additionally, DELETE can be used with TOP to delete only the top portion of records, and is implemented in the same way as Syntax 9-3 (including the use of parenthesis).

9.3 Query Transactions

Transactions are SQL's way of saying "don't commit any changes unless instructed to do so." This has important uses. Imagine a bank customer that has both a checking account and a savings account, and would like to move $2,500 from the checking account to the savings account.

dbo.CheckingAccount		dbo.SavingsAccount	
CustomerName	Balance	CustomerName	Balance
Terry Kraemer	10000	Terry Kraemer	2500

Table 9-7 and Table 9-8

In order to do this, we would need to update his checking account balance by subtracting $2,500 from it, and then update his savings account balance by *adding* $2,500 to it.

```
UPDATE dbo.CheckingAccount
   SET Balance = Balance - 2500
 WHERE CustomerName = 'Terry Kraemer'
```
Query 9-5

And:

```
UPDATE dbo.SavingsAccount
   SET Balance = Balance + 2500
 WHERE CustomerName = 'Terry Kraemer'
```
Query 9-6

Assuming that there are no errors in the code, this is okay. But what happens if Query 9-6 contains code that will generate an error? Imagine that the person who had written the query had accidentally added some invalid code.

```
UPDATE dbo.SavingsAccount
   SET Balance = Balance + 2500/0
 WHERE CustomerName = 'Terry Kraemer'
```
Query 9-7

This will give a divide-by-zero error. But there's more than just that under the surface. After Query 9-5 finishes executing, Terry's checking account balance will be $7,500. When Query 9-7 executes, SQL will fail to add $2,500 to his savings account, meaning Terry just lost $2,500.

That is, unless we use a transaction. Referring back to the top of this chapter, a transaction will keep all changes in limbo until SQL is instructed to commit to them or revert them. Transactions begin with the statement BEGIN TRANSACTION.

```
BEGIN TRANSACTION
     Query(s)
```
Syntax 9-9

In the bank example, we need the balance adjustments for both accounts to function properly, or else we want to undo all of the changes.

```
BEGIN TRANSACTION

UPDATE dbo.CheckingAccount
   SET Balance = Balance - 2500
 WHERE CustomerName = 'Terry Kraemer'

UPDATE dbo.SavingsAccount
   SET Balance = Balance + 2500/0
 WHERE CustomerName = 'Terry Kraemer'
```

Query 9-8

After executing this query, if we followed up by selecting the information from the tables, Terry's checking account balance would read $7,500, and his savings account would still be $2,500. This is not what we want, so we'd have to revert the changes. To do this, we'd use the ROLLBACK command.

```
ROLLBACK
```

Syntax 9-10

Executing the ROLLBACK command by itself will undo the changes that had been introduced since the BEGIN TRANSACTION command. If we roll back the changes and then select the information from the tables again, Terry's savings account balance would still be $2,500, but his checking account balance will have reverted to $10,000.

Imagine that the developer had realized his mistake in Query 9-8, and made the appropriate adjustments to remove the divide-by-zero problem. Now, when the adjusted Query 9-8 is run, Terry's checking and savings balances will be $7,500 and $5,000, respectively. But we have started a transaction, and we're not going to roll it back, so we have to tell SQL to solidify these results in the table. That is done with the COMMIT command.

```
COMMIT
```

Syntax 9-11

Once a transaction has been committed, it cannot be reverted. If a bad change is accidentally committed, it is there to stay unless it is manually reverted.

The COMMIT and ROLLBACK commands both require that a BEGIN TRANSACTION command has been executed before them or else SQL will respond with an error message.

10 Advanced Functionality

10.1 Windowed Aggregate Functions

It was mentioned briefly back in chapter 5.1, but a GROUP BY clause is not always necessary to find out statistical information. Consider the following scenario, you are presented with a table of all customer purchases, and you would like to retrieve the rows for customers who have two or more purchases.

dbo.CustomerPurchases		
CustomerName	PurchaseDate	PurchasePrice
Susan McClung	2020-02-15	43.20
Victor Worcester	2020-02-27	25.68
Angela Aguirre	2020-06-15	50.92
Susan McClung	2020-07-09	12.12
Jon Foster	2020-08-11	94.32
Angela Aguirre	2020-10-30	75.64

Table 10-1

There are two ways to accomplish this that come to mind, an IN list, and an INNER JOIN, but first, a list of the customers who have two or more purchases must be generated. This can be accomplished using the methods outlined in chapter 5.1.

```
    SELECT
DISTINCT CustomerName
    FROM dbo.CustomerPurchases
GROUP BY CustomerName
  HAVING COUNT(*) >= 2
```

Query 10-1

Query Results
CustomerName
Susan McClung
Angela Aguirre

Table 10-2

Now that the query for repeat customers has been created, if an IN list is used to find their information, the approach would be to select the columns from *dbo.CustomerPurchases,* assuming that the customer's name appears in Table 10-2.

```
SELECT CustomerName,
       PurchaseDate,
       PurchasePrice
  FROM dbo.CustomerPurchases
 WHERE CustomerName IN (  SELECT
                        DISTINCT CustomerName
                            FROM dbo.CustomerPurchases
                        GROUP BY CustomerName
                          HAVING COUNT(*) >= 2)
```

Query 10-2

Query Results		
CustomerName	PurchaseDate	PurchasePrice
Susan McClung	2020-02-15	43.20
Angela Aguirre	2020-06-15	50.92
Susan McClung	2020-07-09	12.12
Angela Aguirre	2020-10-30	75.64

Table 10-3

The other possible method is to use an INNER JOIN. We'd select **CustomerName**, **PurchaseDate**, and **PurchasePrice** from Table 10-1 and INNER JOIN it to Table 10-2 with the join criteria on the customer name. This will keep only the customer names that are common between the two tables. And since Table 10-2 only contains the names of repeat customers, we'd end up selecting **CustomerName**, **PurchaseDate**, and **PurchasePrice** for those customer's orders.

```
    SELECT a.CustomerName,
           a.PurchaseDate,
           a.PurchasePrice
      FROM dbo.CustomerPurchases AS a
INNER JOIN (  SELECT
              DISTINCT CustomerName
                  FROM dbo.CustomerPurchases
              GROUP BY CustomerName
                HAVING COUNT(*) >= 2) AS b
        ON a.CustomerName = b.CustomerName
```

Query 10-3

This will produce identical results to Table 10-3.

These methods are not without their drawbacks. If the tables used in the query are small, there's nothing wrong with these approaches to solving the problem. But it's possible that your tables may contain millions, if not billions, of rows each. The larger the table, the longer it takes to compute the results. On top of that, the *dbo.CustomerPurchases* table is being scanned twice; once to find the repeat customers, and once to select their corresponding purchase information. This is an inefficient method, and it can be completed using only one scan of the table.

It is possible to combine window functions with aggregate functions, and at the same time, eliminate the need for a GROUP BY clause. The syntax for a windowed aggregate function is shown in Syntax 10-1.

```
SELECT Columns,
       Aggregate Function(Column) OVER (Window)
  FROM Table
```

Syntax 10-1

There is so much functionality that can fit into the (**Window**) section of the query that it's best if it is demonstrated through examples, each with increasing complexity.

10.1.1 Full Window

The simplest case is a window that encompasses all rows. Suppose that we wanted to take Table 10-1 and display the rows with purchase prices that account for 20% or more of the total revenue (which is $301.89). Using the previous, inefficient method, this would be the following query.

```
SELECT CustomerName,
       PurchaseDate,
       PurchasePrice
  FROM dbo.CustomerPurchases
 WHERE PurchasePrice >= 0.2 * (SELECT SUM(PurchasePrice)
                                 FROM dbo.CustomerPurchases)
```

Query 10-4

A quick calculation shows that 20% of $301.89 is $60.38, meaning any purchase over $60.38 will be displayed.

Query Results		
CustomerName	PurchaseDate	PurchasePrice
Jon Foster	2020-08-11	94.32
Angela Aguirre	2020-10-30	75.64

Table 10-4

But again, this is scanning the same table twice. Instead of having a subquery to calculate the sum of the purchase prices, we can have a new column which displays the sum of the purchase prices.

```
SELECT CustomerName,
       PurchaseDate,
       PurchasePrice,
       SUM(PurchasePrice) OVER () AS SumPurchasePrice
  FROM dbo.CustomerPurchases
```

Query 10-5

The empty parentheses () in this query specify that we are summing the purchase prices across *the entire table*. We are not grouping by any column. This is similar to Query 5-1 which did not contain a GROUP BY clause. Unlike the results from a traditional aggregate function, which is summarized into groups, a windowed aggregate function displays *all rows*, along with an aggregated value.

Query Results			
CustomerName	PurchaseDate	PurchasePrice	SumPurchasePrice
Susan McClung	2020-02-15	43.20	301.89
Victor Worcester	2020-02-27	25.68	301.89
Angela Aguirre	2020-06-15	50.92	301.89
Susan McClung	2020-07-09	12.12	301.89
Jon Foster	2020-08-11	94.32	301.89
Angela Aguirre	2020-10-30	75.64	301.89

Table 10-5

At this point, it seems redundant to have the same exact value repeated for every row. But consider the fact that we were able to retrieve the customer and sum of **PurchasePrice** using only one table scan as opposed to the two scans before. From here, Query 10-5 can be placed into a subquery to solidify the alias of **SumPurchasePrice**, and then filtered to WHERE PurchasePrice >= 0.2 * SumPurchasePrice.

```
SELECT CustomerName,
       PurchaseDate,
       PurchasePrice
  FROM (
        SELECT CustomerName,
               PurchaseDate,
               PurchasePrice,
               SUM(PurchasePrice) OVER () AS SumPurchasePrice
          FROM dbo.CustomerPurchases) AS a
 WHERE PurchasePrice >= 0.2 * SumPurchasePrice
```

Query 10-6

This query will produce the same results as Table 10-4.

10.1.2 Partitioned Window

In the earlier example in chapter 10.1 about customers with two or more purchases, we had to count the number of purchases, grouped by the customer name. Aggregated window functions will allow this operation to be performed as well. In a window function, the PARTITION BY clause is used as a replacement for the GROUP BY clause that would normally be used. The number of purchases per customer can be calculated by using the COUNT(*) function and a PARTITION BY the customer name. The PARTITION BY clause is added inside the parentheses following OVER.

```
SELECT CustomerName,
       PurchaseDate,
       PurchasePrice,
       COUNT(*) OVER (PARTITION BY CustomerName) AS CountPurchases
  FROM dbo.CustomerPurchases
```

Query 10-7

Query Results			
CustomerName	PurchaseDate	PurchasePrice	CountPurchases
Susan McClung	2020-02-15	43.20	2
Victor Worcester	2020-02-27	25.68	1
Angela Aguirre	2020-06-15	50.92	2
Susan McClung	2020-07-09	12.12	2
Jon Foster	2020-08-11	94.32	1
Angela Aguirre	2020-10-30	75.64	2

Table 10-6

Again, this produces some redundant information. Each of Susan's and Angela's two rows show that they have two purchases, but this information was obtained using only one table scan. From here, Query 10-7 can be placed in a subquery to solidify the alias of **CountPurchases**, and then filtered to WHERE CountPurchases >= 2.

```
SELECT CustomerName,
       PurchaseDate,
       PurchasePrice
  FROM (SELECT CustomerName,
               PurchaseDate,
               PurchasePrice,
               COUNT(*) OVER (PARTITION BY CustomerName) AS CountPurchases
          FROM dbo.CustomerPurchases) AS a
 WHERE CountPurchases >= 2
```

Query 10-8

This query will produce the same results as Table 10-3.

10.1.3 Running Totals

Consider the following scenario, you have a table of your bank account information *dbo.BankRecords* (Table 10-7). It contains the dates of your recent transactions, as well as how much the transactions were for.

dbo.BankRecords	
TransactionDate	**TransactionAmount**
2020-05-20	-50.00
2020-05-12	300.00
2020-05-15	-100.00
2020-05-10	500.00
2020-05-25	250.00

Table 10-7

You wish to sort the table in chronological order and find a running total of the balance after each transaction. The inefficient way to do this is to have a correlated subquery. While scanning each row, SQL will look at the date of the transaction (let's say it is currently looking at the 2020-05-15 row), and then calculate the sum of all transactions with a date less than or equal to 2020-05-15.

```
SELECT TransactionDate,
       TransactionAmount,
       (SELECT SUM(TransactionAmount)
          FROM dbo.BankRecords AS b
          WHERE b.TransactionDate <= a.TransactionDate) AS RunningTotal
    FROM dbo.BankRecords AS a
ORDER BY TransactionDate
```

Query 10-9

Query Results		
TransactionDate	**TransactionAmount**	**RunningTotal**
2020-05-10	500.00	500.00
2020-05-12	300.00	800.00
2020-05-15	-100.00	700.00
2020-05-20	-50.00	650.00
2020-05-25	250.00	900.00

Table 10-8

While valid, this method can quickly get out of hand. There is approximately a $1/2\ n^2$ dependency here. The number of calculations done by SQL is about one-half the square of the total number of rows. If the table has ten rows, that's 50 calculations that need to be done. If the table has fifty rows, that's nearly 1,300 calculations that need to be done!

To do this with aggregated window functions, SQL must be told that this data is to be ordered chronologically.

```
SELECT TransactionDate,
       TransactionAmount,
       SUM(TransactionAmount)
         OVER (
           ORDER BY TransactionDate



                ) AS RunningTotal
  FROM dbo.BankRecords
```

Query 10-10

I have left significant whitespace in Query 10-10 because it is still incomplete. We have specified that we want to tackle the data in chronological order, but not which rows to add up. Since this is a running total, we want the sum of all of the prior transactions up to the current row that SQL is processing. We can do so by specifying that we want the ROWS BETWEEN certain limits.

In order to communicate to SQL that we want everything back to the first record, use the phrase UNBOUNDED PRECEDING. And to say that we want to stop at the current row, use CURRENT ROW.

```
SELECT TransactionDate,
       TransactionAmount,
       SUM(TransactionAmount)
         OVER (
           ORDER BY TransactionDate
                ROWS BETWEEN UNBOUNDED PRECEDING
                         AND CURRENT ROW
              ) AS RunningTotal
  FROM dbo.BankRecords
```

Query 10-11

Assuming, again, that we're looking at the 2020-05-15 row, the SUM statement is saying, "order all of the transactions by their date. Then, sum up the transaction amount for every row starting as far back as possible, up to 2020-05-15." Since the data is ordered chronologically, "starting as far back as possible" is the same as summing up all transactions that occurred prior to the current row. This query will produce identical results to Table 10-8.

Partitions can be added into the function, even when using ROWS BETWEEN. Consider the *dbo.BankRecords* table again, except this time, a second customer has been added.

dbo.BankRecords		
CustomerName	TransactionDate	TransactionAmount
Janet Jenkins	2020-05-20	-50.00
Janet Jenkins	2020-05-12	300.00
Janet Jenkins	2020-05-15	-100.00
Janet Jenkins	2020-05-10	500.00
Janet Jenkins	2020-05-25	250.00
Rosa Wade	2020-05-21	15000.00
Rosa Wade	2020-05-13	-3000.00
Rosa Wade	2020-05-16	2000.00
Rosa Wade	2020-05-11	20000.00
Rosa Wade	2020-05-26	-5000.00

Table 10-9

What would happen if we added the customer name column to Query 10-11 but ran it without partitioning based on the customer's name?

Query Results			
CustomerName	TransactionDate	TransactionAmount	RunningTotal
Janet Jenkins	2020-05-10	500.00	500.00
Rosa Wade	2020-05-11	20000.00	20500.00
Janet Jenkins	2020-05-12	300.00	20800.00
Rosa Wade	2020-05-13	-3000.00	17800.00
Janet Jenkins	2020-05-15	-100.00	17700.00
Rosa Wade	2020-05-16	2000.00	19700.00
Janet Jenkins	2020-05-20	-50.00	19650.00
Rosa Wade	2020-05-21	15000.00	34650.00
Janet Jenkins	2020-05-25	250.00	34900.00
Rosa Wade	2020-05-26	-5000.00	29900.00

Table 10-10

One thing is certain, Janet Jenkins is going to be happy with her new-found wealth.

This is a situation in which partitioning is critical.

```
SELECT CustomerName,
       TransactionDate,
       TransactionAmount,
       SUM(TransactionAmount)
         OVER (
           PARTITION BY CustomerName
               ORDER BY TransactionDate
                   ROWS BETWEEN UNBOUNDED PRECEDING
                         AND CURRENT ROW
             ) AS RunningTotal
   FROM dbo.BankRecords
```

Query 10-12

Query Results			
CustomerName	TransactionDate	TransactionAmount	RunningTotal
Janet Jenkins	2020-05-10	500.00	500.00
Janet Jenkins	2020-05-12	300.00	800.00
Janet Jenkins	2020-05-15	-100.00	700.00
Janet Jenkins	2020-05-20	-50.00	650.00
Janet Jenkins	2020-05-25	250.00	900.00
Rosa Wade	2020-05-11	20000.00	20000.00
Rosa Wade	2020-05-13	-3000.00	17000.00
Rosa Wade	2020-05-16	2000.00	19000.00
Rosa Wade	2020-05-21	15000.00	34000.00
Rosa Wade	2020-05-26	-5000.00	29000.00

Table 10-11

After adding a partition, the customer's balances are no longer conflated. Like Query 10-11, SQL will perform the same summing "starting as far back as possible," except it will only go as far back as is possible for the particular customer it happens to be processing. The earliest record in this data set is 2020-05-10, but when SQL is processing Rosa Wade, her "unbounded preceding" record is the one that occurs on 2020-05-11.

10.1.4 Moving Averages, Sums, Counts, etc.

By leveraging ROWS BETWEEN, we can create moving averages, sums, counts, and other aggregated values. We have more options available to us other than just UNBOUNDED PRECEDING and CURRENT ROW.

UNBOUNDED PRECEDING specifies that the window will extend all the way back to the first record in the partition (or table, if no partition is selected).

UNBOUNDED FOLLOWING specifies that the window will extend all the way to the last record in the partition or table.

N PRECEDING, where *N* is a number, specifies that the window will extend to *N* rows prior to the current row.

N FOLLOWING, where *N* is a number, specifies that the window will extend to *N* rows past the current row.

CURRENT ROW specifies that the window will begin or end on the current row.

We will be returning to *dbo.BankRecords*, except we're going to add some additional rows.

dbo.BankRecords	
TransactionDate	**TransactionAmount**
2020-05-20	-50.00
2020-05-12	300.00
2020-05-15	-100.00
2020-05-10	500.00
2020-05-25	250.00
2020-05-30	100.00
2020-06-08	-200.00
2020-06-02	50.00
2020-06-10	-150.00
2020-06-08	150.00

Table 10-12

Using the options for PRECEDING and FOLLOWING shown above, we are going to create a moving average of the transactions to look at the customer's spending habits. We are going to take Query 10-11 and modify it so that the calculated average for each row will be an average of the previous two rows through the following two rows.

```
SELECT TransactionDate,
       TransactionAmount,
       AVG(TransactionAmount)
         OVER (ORDER BY TransactionDate
                    ROWS BETWEEN 2 PRECEDING
                             AND 2 FOLLOWING
              ) AS MovingAverage
  FROM dbo.BankRecords
```

Query 10-13

Query Results		
TransactionDate	TransactionAmount	MovingAverage
2020-05-10	500.00	233.33
2020-05-12	300.00	162.50
2020-05-15	-100.00	180.00
2020-05-20	-50.00	100.00
2020-05-25	250.00	50.00
2020-05-30	100.00	30.00
2020-06-02	50.00	70.00
2020-06-08	-200.00	-10.00
2020-06-08	150.00	-37.50
2020-06-10	-150.00	-66.67

Table 10-13

This same method can be utilized to produce moving sums, moving counts, etc. Similar to chapter 10.1.3, we can add a partition into the query if we need to differentiate on some other factor such as customer name or account number.

10.2 Advanced Grouping Options
10.2.1 Rolling-Up Data

ROLLUP is one way to tell SQL to run the same aggregated query with different grouping levels (thereby emulating running multiple queries, each with a different grouping level). The syntax for ROLLUP is shown below.

```
SELECT Columns,
       Aggregate Function(Column)
   FROM Table
GROUP BY ROLLUP(Columns)
```

Syntax 10-2

Imagine you worked for a school district and were tasked with creating a report that shows the highest SAT[13] score from each class, the highest SAT score from each school, and the highest SAT score in the entire district. Each group becomes more and more generalized; from the very specific classroom-level, to the very general district level. On top of this, all scores need to be displayed in the *same* table.

I've created some sample data in a table called *dbo.DistrictGrades*, shown below. There are three schools in the district, each school has either two or three classes, each class has two or three students, and the student's grade is shown in the right-most column.

dbo.DistrictGrades		
SchoolNumber	ClassNumber	Grade
1	1	1538
1	1	1559
1	2	1487
1	2	1473
1	3	1542
1	3	1511
2	1	1585
2	1	1496
2	1	1486
2	2	1534
2	2	1546
2	2	1569
3	1	1584
3	1	1407
3	2	1494
3	2	1538
3	3	1473
3	3	1411

Table 10-14

To accomplish the task, we can do three queries, grouped at different levels, and then UNION them together. Since UNIONs must have the same number of columns, we must pad the last two queries with null columns to keep the number of columns the same.

---

[13] If you live in the US, you are probably well-acquainted with the SATs. If you are not familiar with it, or live outside of the US, the SAT is our college entrance exam. Generally speaking, better scores open up more opportunities to attend better schools.

```
    SELECT SchoolNumber,
           ClassNumber,
           MAX(Grade) AS MaxGrade
      FROM dbo.DistrictGrades
  GROUP BY SchoolNumber,
           ClassNumber
     UNION
    SELECT SchoolNumber,
           NULL,
           MAX(Grade) AS MaxGrade
      FROM dbo.DistrictGrades
  GROUP BY SchoolNumber
     UNION
    SELECT NULL,
           NULL,
           MAX(Grade) AS MaxGrade
      FROM dbo.DistrictGrades
```

Query 10-14

Query Results		
SchoolNumber	ClassNumber	MaxGrade
1	1	1559
1	2	1487
1	3	1542
2	1	1585
2	2	1569
3	1	1584
3	2	1538
3	3	1473
1	NULL	1559
2	NULL	1585
3	NULL	1584
NULL	NULL	1585

Table 10-15

I have added the thick borders to help distinguish which rows come from which query. The first eight rows are displaying the maximum grade per class per school. The next three rows come from the second query, which is grouped by **SchoolNumber** only. These rows represent the maximum grade per school. The nulls in the 2nd column were manually placed in the query. The final row comes from the third query, which was not grouped at all. This row represents the maximum grade of the entire district. The nulls in the 1st and 2nd column were also manually placed in the query.

As we go down, the grouping gets more generalized. The grouping begins to "step-down" as we pick off the last item in the GROUP BY list in each subsequent query.

While this query works, the problem is that the table will be scanned as many times as there are different groups (three different levels of grouping, three queries, three table scans). Instead of writing three different queries with three different grouping levels, ROLLUP will automatically perform the same "stepping-down."

Using ROLLUP, we can rewrite Query 10-14 in a much simpler form.

```
  SELECT SchoolNumber,
         ClassNumber,
         MAX(Grade) AS MaxGrade
    FROM dbo.DistrictGrades
GROUP BY ROLLUP(SchoolNumber, ClassNumber)
```

Query 10-15

This query will start by selecting the max grade grouped by **SchoolNumber** and **ClassNumber**. Then it will select the max grade grouped by **SchoolNumber** only. Finally, it will select the max grade without any grouping, and it will combine all of the rows into one result set. It will also automatically handle the placement of null values like we did in Query 10-14. The query will generate results identical to Table 10-15.

10.2.2 Cubing Data

CUBE is similar to ROLLUP in that it will automatically calculate aggregate values with different grouping levels, but CUBE takes it one step further.

```
SELECT Columns,
       Aggregate Function(Column)
  FROM Table
GROUP BY CUBE(Columns)
```

Syntax 10-3

We saw with ROLLUP that the grouping level gets more and more general by picking the last column off of the GROUP BY clause and then calculating the aggregate value. This leaves us with some groups that are never explored. We calculated grouping by **SchoolNumber** and **ClassNumber**, and then by **SchoolNumber** alone, but never by **ClassNumber** alone. This is the purpose of CUBE. It will generate all permutations of groups, whereas ROLLUP simply removed the last column in the list with each iteration. To change Query 10-15 to utilize CUBE, we need only change the keyword.

```
SELECT SchoolNumber,
       ClassNumber,
       MAX(Grade) AS MaxGrade
  FROM dbo.DistrictGrades
GROUP BY CUBE(SchoolNumber, ClassNumber)
```

Query 10-16

Query Results

SchoolNumber	ClassNumber	MaxGrade
1	1	1559
1	2	1487
1	3	1542
2	1	1585
2	2	1569
3	1	1584
3	2	1538
3	3	1473
1	NULL	1559
2	NULL	1585
3	NULL	1584
NULL	1	1585
NULL	2	1569
NULL	3	1542
NULL	NULL	1585

Table 10-16

Thick borders have again been added for emphasis. There are three additional rows in this table that were not present in Table 10-15. These represent the permutations that were not calculated by ROLLUP, which is the grouping by **ClassNumber** only. The first class's max grade of 1585 was calculated by looking at the grades from first class at the first school, the first class at the second school, and the first class at the third school, and picking the highest one.

10.2.3 Choosing More Than One Group

The last of the advanced grouping capabilities is GROUPING SETS, which takes elements from both ROLLUP and CUBE, as well as the standard GROUP BY. It is similar to ROLLUP and CUBE in that multiple levels of aggregation can be achieved without scanning a table multiple times, but similar to a standard GROUP BY in that the levels of aggregation must be explicitly stated. GROUPING SETS will *not* automatically calculate any permutations that are not listed.

```
SELECT Columns,
       Aggregate Function(Column)
   FROM Table
GROUP BY GROUPING SETS(Columns)
```

Syntax 10-4

Inside the parentheses after GROUPING SETS, the desired levels of aggregation are listed. Referring back to the SAT scores example, we can display the max scores grouped only by **SchoolNumber**, as well as the max scores grouped only by **ClassNumber**. As shown in the earlier examples, SQL will handle the placement of null values automatically.

```
SELECT SchoolNumber,
       ClassNumber,
       MAX(Grade) AS MaxGrade
   FROM dbo.DistrictGrades
GROUP BY GROUPING SETS(SchoolNumber, ClassNumber)
```

Query 10-17

Query Results		
SchoolNumber	ClassNumber	MaxGrade
1	NULL	1559
2	NULL	1585
3	NULL	1584
NULL	1	1585
NULL	2	1569
NULL	3	1542

Table 10-17

Since only **SchoolNumber** and **ClassNumber** were listed, they are the only levels that are grouped by in the results. Suppose next we wanted two different grouping sets, the first of which is grouped by both **SchoolNumber** *and* **ClassNumber** (i.e., GROUP BY SchoolNumber, ClassNumber), and the second is the grand maximum score of the entire data set (i.e., not grouped by anything).

This presents a bit of a problem, how do we represent grouping by multiple columns, as well as grouping by *no* columns? The solution to both is to use a pair of parentheses. Any time there is a grouping set that utilizes multiple columns, the group will need to be enclosed within parentheses. Likewise, grand totals, grand maximums, grand minimums, etc. are denoted by an empty set of parentheses.

```
SELECT SchoolNumber,
       ClassNumber,
       MAX(Grade) AS MaxGrade
  FROM dbo.DistrictGrades
GROUP BY GROUPING SETS( (SchoolNumber, ClassNumber), () )
```

Query 10-18

SchoolNumber	ClassNumber	MaxGrade
1	1	1559
1	2	1487
1	3	1542
2	1	1585
2	2	1569
3	1	1584
3	2	1538
3	3	1473
NULL	NULL	1585

Query Results

Table 10-18

A thick border has been added to distinguish which rows come from each grouping set.

10.3 Update Using a Join

It is not always the case that an UPDATE statement will be a simple operation. In chapter 9.1.1, we increased the value of **Grade** by five. We could have also set it to a specific grade. In either case, *dbo.ExamGrades* was the only table present in the UPDATE statement. But what if the information we want lies in another table? How would we connect the two tables? SQL Server has the ability to invoke more than one table during an update. Syntax 10-5 shows how to use a JOIN in an UPDATE statement.

```
    UPDATE Fact Alias
       SET Column = Value
      FROM Fact Table AS Fact Alias
Type JOIN Dimension Table AS Dim Alias
        ON Foreign Key = Primary Key
```

Syntax 10-5

When invoking more than one table, instead of writing UPDATE **Table**, replace the name of the table with an alias. The UPDATE statement continues normally with setting the value of a column to a different value. But the FROM statement is where we really start to deviate from the norm. After the FROM clause, we list our table name along with the alias we chose on the first line. From here, we can create a JOIN statement like we normally would.

Returning back to the first example in chapter 9.1.1, suppose that instead of adding five to everyone's grade, we had specific values that we wanted to update them to which were stored in a separate table. I have reproduced part of Table 9-1 as the table we want to update, and I have introduced *dbo.NewGrades* as the table we would like to source the updated data from. Notice that the grades listed in *dbo.NewGrades* are not simply increments of the grades in *dbo.ExamGrades*.

dbo.ExamGrades		dbo.NewGrades	
Student	**Grade**	**Student**	**Grade**
Melissa Manns	76	Melissa Manns	84
Douglas Hayes	94	Douglas Hayes	95
Thomas Theodore	88	Thomas Theodore	88

Table 10-19 and Table 10-20

Using Syntax 10-5, we can build our UPDATE statement. We'll alias *dbo.ExamGrades* as "OldGrades," and alias *dbo.NewGrades* as "NewGrades." We will also JOIN the two tables together on the student name.

```
    UPDATE OldGrades
       SET OldGrades.Grade = NewGrades.Grade
      FROM dbo.ExamGrades AS OldGrades
LEFT JOIN dbo.ExamGrades AS NewGrades
        ON OldGrades.Student = NewGrades.Student
```

Query 10-19

After running Query 10-19, *dbo.ExamGrades* (Table 10-21) will reflect the grades seen in *dbo.NewGrades*.

dbo.ExamGrades	
Student	**Grade**
Melissa Manns	84
Douglas Hayes	95
Thomas Theodore	88

Table 10-21

I chose a LEFT JOIN for Query 10-19, but any JOIN type would have worked in this scenario. Also, we are not limited to joins. We can utilize an OUTER APPLY if we so choose. We would only have to change the syntax to match that shown in chapter 8.5.

10.4 Update From a Subquery

It was mentioned back in chapter 6.1 that window functions could not be placed in a WHERE clause. This poses a problem. Consider our table of student grades from chapter 3.7 (reproduced).

dbo.ExamGrades	
Student	**Grade**
Gina Melvin	76
Donny Wilmoth	76
Barbara Fisher	99
John Fleck	77
Clayton Wheeler	88
Robert Harris	84
Kenneth Copeland	50
Christine Cox	33
Robert Ruhl	36
Billy Hill	49

Table 10-22

How could we execute an UPDATE statement such as the following one, which updates students with a rank less than or equal to three?

```
UPDATE dbo.ExamGrades
   SET Grade = Grade + 1
 WHERE RANK() OVER (ORDER BY Grade DESC) <= 3
```

Query 10-20

The solution is to use a subquery. Much like updating a table via a JOIN, the syntax for the typical UPDATE statement must be adjusted with an alias instead of the table name after UPDATE.

```
UPDATE Alias
   SET Column = Value
 FROM (Subquery) AS Alias
```

Syntax 10-6

Since window functions cannot be used in a WHERE clause, we can insert a subquery that creates a dedicated rank column, and then the remainder of the UPDATE statement filters on the rank column.

```
UPDATE OldGrades
   SET Grade = Grade + 1
  FROM (SELECT Student,
               Grade,
               RANK() OVER (ORDER BY Grade DESC) AS GradeRank
          FROM dbo.ExamGrades) AS OldGrades
 WHERE GradeRank <= 3
```

Query 10-21

After executing Query 10-21, the top-ranking students will have their grades incremented by one (Table 10-23).

dbo.ExamGrades	
Student	**Grade**
Gina Melvin	76
Donny Wilmoth	76
Barbara Fisher	100
John Fleck	77
Clayton Wheeler	89
Robert Harris	85
Kenneth Copeland	50
Christine Cox	33
Robert Ruhl	36
Billy Hill	49

Table 10-23

10.5 Delete Using a Join

Just like an UPDATE statement, we are able to delete rows from one table depending on the values in another table. The syntax, too, is slightly different from a normal DELETE command.

```
DELETE Fact Alias
    FROM Fact Table AS Fact Alias
Type JOIN Dimension Table AS Dim Alias
      ON Foreign Key = Primary Key
```

Syntax 10-7

We'll revisit the tables and examples from chapter 10.3. I have reproduced the earlier tables.

dbo.ExamGrades			dbo.NewGrades	
Student	**Grade**		**Student**	**Grade**
Melissa Manns	76		Melissa Manns	84
Douglas Hayes	94		Douglas Hayes	95
Thomas Theodore	88		Thomas Theodore	88

Table 10-24 and Table 10-25

This time, instead of updating *dbo.ExamGrades* based on the values in *dbo.NewGrades*, we will be *deleting* values from *dbo.ExamGrades* based on the values in *dbo.NewGrades*. Suppose that we wanted to delete rows from *dbo.ExamGrades* if the student's grade in *dbo.NewGrades* is less than 90.

Like Query 10-19, instead of starting with DELETE and then the table name, the table is replaced with an alias, and is followed up by FROM, and then a JOIN statement. The join criteria will be the same, the student's names. The main difference in this new query is that we are adding a WHERE clause. This isn't strictly necessary, but without it, the DELETE command will wipe an entire table clear. Most of Query 10-19 can be reused, and adjusted where necessary.

```
DELETE OldGrades
    FROM dbo.ExamGrades AS OldGrades
LEFT JOIN dbo.ExamGrades AS NewGrades
      ON OldGrades.Student = NewGrades.Student
   WHERE NewGrades.Grade < 90
```

Query 10-22

After running this query, *dbo.ExamGrades* will now only list one student, Douglas Hayes. His new grade was above a 90, so he was not deleted.

dbo.ExamGrades	
Student	**Grade**
Douglas Hayes	94

Table 10-26

10.6 Delete From a Subquery

Like updating using a subquery, DELETE statements can make use of subqueries. In cases where you wish to delete based off of a window function, a subquery must be used to create an actual column, and then the deleting is done based off of that column.

Using Table 10-22 again, how could we execute a DELETE statement such as the one below?

```
DELETE FROM dbo.ExamGrades
WHERE RANK() OVER (ORDER BY Grade DESC) = 1
```
Query 10-23

Again, the solution is to use a subquery. The syntax must be adjusted to use an alias after DELETE.

```
DELETE Alias
  FROM (Subquery) AS Alias
```
Syntax 10-8

To delete based off of a window function, the window function must appear in the subquery.

```
DELETE GradeQuery
  FROM (SELECT Student,
               Grade,
               RANK() OVER (ORDER BY Grade DESC) AS GradeRank
        FROM dbo.ExamGrades) AS GradeQuery
 WHERE GradeRank = 1
```
Query 10-24

After executing Query 10-24, the top-scoring student will be deleted from the table (Table 10-27).

dbo.ExamGrades	
Student	**Grade**
Gina Melvin	76
Donny Wilmoth	76
John Fleck	77
Clayton Wheeler	88
Robert Harris	84
Kenneth Copeland	50
Christine Cox	33
Robert Ruhl	36
Billy Hill	49

Table 10-27

10.7 Merging Two Tables Together

Merging two tables is a method of deleting, updating, and inserting in one step. Consider the following scenario, an internet provider offers four tiers of service, each with increasing speed. Their products are shown in Table 10-28 along with the speed of the internet service in Megabits per second (Mbps).

dbo.InternetServices		
ProductID	ProductName	InternetSpeed
1	Basic	10
2	Plus	20
3	Premier	50
4	Super	100

Table 10-28

But after several years, the need for faster internet speeds is rising, and the demand for low-speed services is dropping. The company decides to add a new tier called "Ultimate" which is 200 Mbps, and drop the basic tier, as it is too slow. Additionally, any other existing tiers are given a boost of 20 Mbps. The proposed new tiers are shown in Table 10-29.

dbo.ProposedServices			
ProductID	ProductName	CurrentSpeed	ProposedSpeed
2	Plus	20	40
3	Premier	50	70
4	Super	100	120
5	Ultimate	NULL	200

Table 10-29

The task is to now update *dbo.InternetServices* with the information in *dbo.ProposedServices*, as well as insert and delete rows where necessary. If we were to use the existing methods that we've learned so far, this would be three separate commands: a DELETE, an UPDATE, and an INSERT. These can be simplified into one statement using the MERGE command.

```
MERGE Target Table AS TARGET
USING Source Table AS SOURCE
ON TARGET.Target Key
 = SOURCE.Source Key

WHEN MATCHED THEN
Update/Insert/Delete

WHEN NOT MATCHED BY TARGET THEN
Update/Insert/Delete

WHEN NOT MATCHED BY SOURCE THEN
Update/Insert/Delete;
```

Syntax 10-9

This the most complicated syntax we've dealt with. Once we break it down, we'll see that it's an intuitive way of accomplishing the tasks at hand. First, the TARGET and SOURCE tables must be defined. The table that is operated upon (*dbo.InternetServices*) is the target table. The table that the new data is drawn from (*dbo.ProposedServices*) is the source table. **ProductID** from both tables can be used to link them together. Query 10-25 shows the status of the query so far.

```
MERGE dbo.InternetServices AS TARGET
USING dbo.ProposedServices AS SOURCE
ON TARGET.ProductID = SOURCE.ProductID

WHEN MATCHED THEN
Update/Insert/Delete

WHEN NOT MATCHED BY TARGET THEN
Update/Insert/Delete

WHEN NOT MATCHED BY SOURCE THEN
Update/Insert/Delete;
```

Query 10-25

The following two tables show the matching between them based on the join criteria. The target table has a product ID (the basic tier) which has no matching product ID in the source table, and the source table has a product ID (the ultimate tier) which has no matching product ID in the target table.

dbo.InternetServices (TARGET)			dbo.ProposedServices (SOURCE)			
ProductID	ProductName	InternetSpeed	ProductID	ProductName	CurrentSpeed	ProposedSpeed
1	Basic	10	Not matched by source			
2	Plus	20	2	Plus	20	40
3	Premier	50	3	Premier	50	70
4	Super	100	4	Super	100	120
Not matched by target			5	Ultimate	NULL	200

Table 10-30 and Table 10-31

We will use this information to finish the query.

WHEN MATCHED THEN instructs SQL what to do in the event that there is a match on the join criteria.

WHEN NOT MATCHED BY TARGET instructs SQL what to do in the event that a row does not exist in the target table, but *does* exist in the source table (the ultimate tier of service).

WHEN NOT MATCHED BY SOURCE instructs SQL what to do in the event that a row exists in the target table, but *does not* exist in the source table (the basic tier of service).

Let's recap what we want to do:

- If the tiers match between the two tables, update the speed in *dbo.InternetServices* to reflect the proposed speed in *dbo.ProposedServices*.
- If a tier exists in *dbo.InternetServices*, but does not exist in *dbo.ProposedServices*, delete it from *dbo.InternetServices*.
- If a tier exists in *dbo.ProposedServices* but does not exist in *dbo.InternetServices*, add it to *dbo.InternetServices*.

This would finalize the MERGE statement to Query 10-26.

```
MERGE dbo.InternetServices AS TARGET
USING dbo.ProposedServices AS SOURCE
ON TARGET.ProductID = SOURCE.ProductID

WHEN MATCHED THEN
UPDATE
SET TARGET.InternetSpeed = SOURCE.ProposedSpeed

WHEN NOT MATCHED BY TARGET THEN
INSERT (ProductID, ProductName, InternetSpeed)
VALUES (SOURCE.ProductID, SOURCE.ProductName, SOURCE.ProposedSpeed)

WHEN NOT MATCHED BY SOURCE THEN
DELETE;
```

Query 10-26

This is another scenario in which a semicolon is required after the entire statement. After executing this query, the original table, *dbo.InternetServices* will reflect the changes made by the query. The results are shown in Table 10-32.

dbo.InternetServices		
ProductID	ProductName	InternetSpeed
2	Plus	40
3	Premier	70
4	Super	120
5	Ultimate	200

Table 10-32

The syntax of the UPDATE, INSERT, and DELETE statements in Query 10-26 don't quite match the usual syntax shown in earlier chapters. All three statements are missing the name of the table. In this case, the name of the table is unnecessary. Since *dbo.InternetServices* was declared as the target table, it is implied that any update, insert, or delete operation is to be carried out on said table.

10.8 Outputting Results From Update and Delete

After performing an operation that alters data, we normally don't care about what the data *used* to be, only what it is now. This isn't always the case. Perhaps we delete data from a table, but want to view exactly what was deleted or maybe even retain the old values in a separate table in case we need to perform an audit in the future. This is a simple procedure that can be done in several steps, but why perform more steps when you can accomplish it in only one?

By using the OUTPUT command, SQL will delete rows from a table according to the DELETE statement, and then display the rows that were deleted.

```
DELETE FROM Table
OUTPUT DELETED.Columns
```

Syntax 10-10

Immediately after OUTPUT, list the individual columns that will be reviewed (much like how you'd compose a select statement), each aliased with DELETED. All of the columns can be selected with OUTPUT DELETED.*.

I've created a new table named *dbo.EmployeeInfo* which contains the names and ID numbers of employees at a company.

dbo.EmployeeInfo	
ID_Num	FullName
5	Kathryn Duke
2	Michael Bell
7	Julia Ryan
6	Kisha Marti
3	Jason Hilbert
1	Cesar Lauer
4	Vicky Burling
9	Marco Ramos
8	Linda Amin

Table 10-33

Suppose we wanted to delete all employees whose ID number is greater than five, and then display both **FullName** and **ID_Num** for those affected.

```
DELETE FROM dbo.EmployeeInfo
OUTPUT DELETED.*
 WHERE ID_Num > 5
```

Query 10-27

Query Results	
ID_Num	FullName
7	Julia Ryan
6	Kisha Marti
9	Marco Ramos
8	Linda Amin

Table 10-34

These rows represent the rows that were deleted from the table. To verify this, if we select the data from the original table, we will have fewer rows remaining.

dbo.EmployeeInfo	
ID_Num	FullName
5	Kathryn Duke
2	Michael Bell
3	Jason Hilbert
1	Cesar Lauer
4	Vicky Burling

Table 10-35

Let's take one step back and imagine that we hadn't just run Query 10-27, and that *dbo.EmployeeInfo* table still contains its original data. Suppose we want to perform the same action, delete employees with an ID number greater than five, but instead, we don't need to know what the ID number was, we only want their name.

```
DELETE FROM dbo.EmployeeInfo
OUTPUT DELETED.FullName
 WHERE ID_Num > 5
```

Query 10-28

After executing Query 10-28, we will be presented with the same results as Table 10-34, albeit without **ID_Num**. Outputting only certain columns in no way affects the delete functionality of the query.

The ability to see the data that was deleted is a good start, but it is also fleeting. If the window is closed, or another query is executed, the information about the deleted rows is gone. To get around this, we can instruct SQL to store the rows that were deleted in a new or existing table.

Once again, imagine that we had not deleted any rows from the *dbo.EmployeeInfo* table. We will perform the same delete operation on the table, except this time, the rows that are deleted from *dbo.EmployeeInfo* will be inserted into a pre-existing and empty table named *dbo.OldEmployeeInfo*, which has identical columns to *dbo.EmployeeInfo*.

To specify that the deleted rows should be stored somewhere, use INTO. Query 10-28 will be modified to include INTO, as well as the table we want the rows moved to.

```
DELETE FROM dbo.EmployeeInfo
OUTPUT DELETED.*
  INTO dbo.OldEmployeeInfo
 WHERE ID_Num > 5
```

Query 10-29

After executing this query, if we select all of the rows from *dbo.OldEmployeeInfo*, we will find that it is identical to Table 10-34.

The output command is not limited to when data is deleted. It can also be used with insert, UPDATE, and MERGE statements. In an UPDATE statement, the OUTPUT clause goes after the SET command, but before the WHERE clause. When OUTPUT is used in an UPDATE statement, there are two possible values to display. The first is the value of a field *before* being updated, the second is the value of a field *after* being updated.

Returning again to Table 10-33, suppose we wanted to update **ID_Num** for each employee such that it is incremented by one, and then display the employee name, along with both their original and updated **ID_Num** field. The original value of a column and the updated value of a column are referred to as DELETED.*Column* and INSERTED.*Column* respectively. Therefore, to update the data and view the original and updated **ID_Num** values, the following query would be used (the column **FullName** can be either the DELETED or INSERTED version since it isn't altered).

```
UPDATE dbo.EmployeeInfo
   SET ID_Num = ID_Num + 1
OUTPUT DELETED.FullName,
       DELETED.ID_Num,
       INSERTED.ID_Num
```

Query 10-30

Query Results		
FullName	ID_Num	ID_Num
Kathryn Duke	5	6
Michael Bell	2	3
Julia Ryan	7	8
Kisha Marti	6	7
Jason Hilbert	3	4
Cesar Lauer	1	2
Vicky Burling	4	5
Marco Ramos	9	10
Linda Amin	8	9

Table 10-36

To someone who didn't know the structure of the query beforehand, these results might be confusing. Which column is the old **ID_Num** and which one is the updated one? Like a normal SELECT statement, the results of OUTPUT can be aliased. The last line of Query 10-30 may read:

```
OUTPUT DELETED.FullName, DELETED.ID_Num AS Old_ID, INSERTED.ID_Num AS New_ID
```

10.9 Pivoting Data

A pivot table is a way of arranging and summarizing data to calculate sums, averages, or other statistical figures. Consider the following table, *dbo.ApplianceSales* which shows the purchases made at a department store for various appliances.

dbo.ApplianceSales		
PurchaseDate	Appliance	PurchasePrice
2020-04-18	Toaster	20.00
2020-04-19	Refrigerator	540.00
2020-04-19	Microwave	90.00
2020-04-18	Refrigerator	770.00
2020-04-18	Microwave	110.00
2020-04-19	Microwave	70.00
2020-04-18	Refrigerator	650.00
2020-04-18	Microwave	50.00
2020-04-18	Toaster	30.00
2020-04-19	Toaster	35.00

Table 10-37

Suppose we wanted to calculate the sum of **PurchasePrice** for each appliance type on each day. Using what we've learned so far, one possible way to do this is to select **PurchaseDate**, **Appliance**, and the sum of **PurchasePrice** from this table, grouped by **PurchaseDate** and **Appliance**. Such a query would generate the following table.

Query Results		
PurchaseDate	Appliance	SumPurchasePrice
2020-04-18	Microwave	160.00
2020-04-18	Refrigerator	1420.00
2020-04-18	Toaster	50.00
2020-04-19	Microwave	160.00
2020-04-18	Refrigerator	540.00
2020-04-18	Toaster	35.00

Table 10-38

Using the GROUP BY clause, the layout of this report is the only option we have. But what if we desired a layout like the one shown in Table 10-39? Instead of Microwave, Refrigerator, and Toaster being distributed amongst several rows within the same column, they now each have their own column. In situations like this, we say that **Appliance** was *pivoted*.

Query Results			
PurchaseDate	Microwave	Refrigerator	Toaster
2020-04-18	160.00	1420.00	50.00
2020-04-19	160.00	540.00	35.00

Table 10-39

One option is to use Query 10-31. Each sum has a CASE statement inside which will only add the **PurchasePrice** to the total if the appliance matches the type given in the condition. If the appliance type does not match, the CASE statement will evaluate to null, and **PurchasePrice** for that particular sum will be disregarded. If a row has a toaster as the appliance, then **PurchasePrice** would be ignored for the first and second sum statements, but summed for the third one.

```
    SELECT PurchaseDate,
           SUM(CASE WHEN Appliance = 'Microwave'
                    THEN PurchasePrice END) AS Microwave,
           SUM(CASE WHEN Appliance = 'Refrigerator'
                    THEN PurchasePrice END) AS Refrigerator,
           SUM(CASE WHEN Appliance = 'Toaster'
                    THEN PurchasePrice END) AS Toaster
      FROM dbo.ApplianceSales
GROUP BY PurchaseDate
ORDER BY PurchaseDate
```

Query 10-31

An alternative method is to use PIVOT. The syntax for PIVOT is shown below.

```
SELECT Regular Columns,
       Pivoted Columns
  FROM (
        SELECT Columns
        FROM Table
       ) AS Table Alias
  PIVOT (
        Aggregate Function(Column) FOR
        Column To Pivot IN (Values To Pivot)
       ) AS Pivot Alias
```

Syntax 10-11

The syntax for a PIVOT query can be a little confusing, but with some practice, you'll quickly be able to grasp how to leverage it to your advantage. We'll start out of order, and tackle the subquery inside the FROM clause first. In this subquery, select the columns from the original table that will be required to create the pivoted table. If all columns in a table are used, it is not necessary to use a subquery, but we'll continue to do so for this example. We are aiming to recreate Table 10-39 using Table 10-37, which requires all three columns, **PurchaseDate**, **Appliance** (which will be pivoted), and the **PurchasePrice** (which will be summed). Be sure to alias the subquery/table.

```
SELECT Regular Columns,
       Pivoted Columns
  FROM (
        SELECT PurchaseDate,
               Appliance,
               PurchasePrice
          FROM dbo.ApplianceSales
       ) AS A
  PIVOT (
        Aggregate Function(Column) FOR
        Column To Pivot IN (Values To Pivot)
       ) AS Pivot Alias
```

Query 10-32

Next, we'll discuss the PIVOT query. The goal is to have summed-price columns for each individual appliance, so our aggregate function will be SUM(PurchasePrice). *Values to pivot* are the actual values that will each become their own column; **Microwave, Refrigerator**, and **Toaster**. *Column to pivot* is the column which contains said values; **Appliance**. Important to note, the *Values to pivot* must be individually wrapped in square brackets. You should also alias the PIVOT subquery.

```
SELECT Regular Columns,
       Pivoted Columns
  FROM (
        SELECT PurchaseDate,
               Appliance,
               PurchasePrice
          FROM dbo.ApplianceSales
       ) AS A
  PIVOT (
         SUM(PurchasePrice) FOR
         Appliance IN ([Microwave], [Refrigerator], [Toaster])
        ) AS P
```

Query 10-33

Lastly, select the names of the columns in the final result set. The *regular columns* are those which were not pivoted or involved in the pivoting (**PurchaseDate**). The pivoted columns are those which were created via the PIVOT query (**Microwave, Refrigerator**, and **Toaster**). The query is now complete.

```
SELECT PurchaseDate,
       Microwave,
       Refrigerator,
       Toaster
  FROM (
        SELECT PurchaseDate,
               Appliance,
               PurchasePrice
          FROM dbo.ApplianceSales
       ) AS A
  PIVOT (
         SUM(PurchasePrice) FOR
         Appliance IN ([Microwave], [Refrigerator], [Toaster])
        ) AS P
```

Query 10-34

When this query is executed, it will be identical to Table 10-39.

One of the downsides to the PIVOT method (and the earlier CASE WHEN Appliance = ... method) is that the user must know beforehand what values appear in the column that will be pivoted. If a row is inserted with a new appliance such as a blender, and the query is not modified to reflect this, the column for blenders will not automatically appear in the result set.

It is possible to write a query which will dynamically generate a list of values and pivot the table, but it is a sloppy and complicated solution involving casting your entire query as one long string and executing it. This approach will not be covered in this book. If you still wish to learn about this method, do a web search for "SQL pivot dynamic" for websites with tutorials on how to accomplish this.

10.10 Unpivoting Data

The opposite process of pivoting is possible, too. Suppose we start with data that has already been summed as shown in Table 10-39, and would like to convert it to the layout shown in Table 10-38. This would be an UNPIVOT operation.

```
  SELECT Regular Columns,
         Unpivoted Columns
    FROM Table AS Table Alias
UNPIVOT (
         Metric Column FOR
         Column From Unpivot IN (Values To Unpivot)
         ) AS Unpivot Alias
```
Syntax 10-12

We will start with Table 10-39 and give it the name *dbo.UnpivotExample*.

dbo.UnpivotExample			
PurchaseDate	Microwave	Refrigerator	Toaster
2020-04-18	160.00	1420.00	50.00
2020-04-19	160.00	540.00	35.00

Table 10-40

```
  SELECT Regular Columns,
         Unpivoted Columns
    FROM dbo.UnpivotExample AS A
UNPIVOT (
         Metric Column FOR
         Column From Unpivot IN (Values To Unpivot)
         ) AS Unpivot Alias
```
Query 10-35

Metric column is the desired name of the single column that all of the metric values will be placed into. The values of $160, $1,420, $50, etc. will reside within this column. Since this column was originally named **PurchasePrice**, that will be the chosen name.

```
  SELECT Regular Columns,
         Unpivoted Columns
    FROM dbo.UnpivotExample AS A
UNPIVOT (
         PurchasePrice FOR
         Column From Unpivot IN (Values To Unpivot)
         ) AS Unpivot Alias
```
Query 10-36

Values to unpivot are the actual column headers that will become their own rows. Since *dbo.UnpivotExample* has columns for **Microwave**, **Refrigerator**, and **Toaster** (and we want these to be distributed amongst rows instead of columns), these three will be the values. **Column from unpivot** is the desired name of the new column that will contain those values. Since they were originally contained in a column named **Appliance**, we will reuse this name.

146

```
SELECT Regular Columns,
       Unpivoted Columns
  FROM dbo.UnpivotExample AS A
UNPIVOT (
         PurchasePrice FOR
         Appliance IN ([Microwave], [Refrigerator], [Toaster])
         ) AS U
```

Query 10-37

Lastly, the *regular columns* are those which were not unpivoted or involved in the unpivoting (**PurchaseDate**), and *unpivoted columns* are those which were created via the UNPIVOT query (**Appliance**, and **PurchasePrice**).

```
SELECT PurchaseDate,
       Appliance,
       PurchasePrice
  FROM dbo.UnpivotExample AS A
UNPIVOT (
         PurchasePrice FOR
         Appliance IN ([Microwave], [Refrigerator], [Toaster])
         ) AS U
```

Query 10-38

The results of Query 10-38 will be identical to Table 10-38.

10.11 Identity Columns

It was mentioned back in chapter 2.5 that when inserting values into a table, the number of values listed is generally equal to the number of columns in the target table. This is not always the case. We can create what is known as an identity column. When creating a table, an identity column is given two parameters, the starting (or seed) value, and an increment value. When inserting the first record, the value of the identity column for that row will be the seed value. When inserting the next row, the value of the identity column will be the seed value plus the increment value. Every subsequent row will add the increment value again.

We will return to Query 2-1 to create the table *dbo.PersonInformation*, except this time, we will also include an identity column.

```
CREATE TABLE dbo.PersonInformation
(
       ID int IDENTITY(1,1),
       PersonName varchar(20) NOT NULL,
       Age int NULL,
       BirthDate date NULL
) ON [PRIMARY]
```
Query 10-39

The first column, **ID**, is given a data type as it normally would, and then it is immediately followed by IDENTITY(1,1). Naturally, the phrase IDENTITY is required to tell SQL that it is an identity column, and (1,1) tells SQL what the seed (initial value) and the increment are.

After executing the query, the table will be created with four columns. To insert a record, we can reuse Query 2-2 (reproduced).

```
INSERT INTO dbo.PersonInformation
     VALUES ('John Doe', 38, '1980-01-01')
```
Query 10-40

Despite there being fewer values listed in Query 10-40 than there are columns in *dbo.PersonInformation*, SQL does not give us an error when executing the query. This is because the identity column is automatically assigned a value when a record is inserted. SQL does not allow the inserting of explicit values into identity columns unless it is told to allow them, but that is above the level of this book.

After executing this query, the table will contain one record, with an identity value automatically assigned.

dbo.PersonInformation			
ID	PersonName	Age	BirthDate
1	John Doe	38	1980-01-01

Table 10-41

If we go on to reuse Query 2-3, each additional row will be incremented by one.

dbo.PersonInformation			
ID	PersonName	Age	BirthDate
1	Jane Doe	20	1998-02-01
2	John Q Public	25	1993-03-01
3	John Doe	38	1980-01-01

Table 10-42

The rows are starting from one and incrementing by one because that is how the column was originally defined. Had the column been created as IDENTITY(1,2), the three rows would have instead been one, three and five. Had the column been declared as (2,3), the three rows would have been two, five, and eight.

It is important to know how the numbering scheme functions with an identity column. If we deleted the last row in Table 10-42 (John Doe with **ID** = 3) and then later inserted a new row, the new row *would not* have **ID** = 3, but rather **ID** = 4.

If we deleted the second row (John Q Public with **ID** = 2) instead of the third row, and then inserted a new row, the new row *would not* have **ID** = 2. It would also have **ID** = 4.

Other than the ability to generate a row number, what is the use of an identity column? Since the identity column will never reuse a value, it is useful for generating unique key values, which aids in making sure that the joins don't run up against duplicate key values (chapter 8.4.4).

10.12 Variables

A common scenario when querying against multiple tables is that they all need to be filtered to the same value, e.g.:

```
SELECT Columns
  FROM 1st Table
 WHERE SaleDate = '2021-01-14'
 UNION
SELECT Columns
  FROM 2nd Table
 WHERE SaleDate = '2021-01-14'
 UNION
SELECT Columns
  FROM 3rd Table
 WHERE SaleDate = '2021-01-14'
```

Syntax 10-13

However, this becomes a pain once it's time to change the filter condition, such as changing Jan. 14th, 2021 to Jan. 15th, 2021. This is where using variables becomes convenient. A variable is declared using the following syntax.

```
DECLARE @Variable Name    Data Type
```

Syntax 10-14

The variable name *must* include the "at" symbol, @, as the first character. Similar to when creating a table, the data type must be given. As an example, to create a `date` variable named "SaleDate," the query would be the following (and it goes without saying that this method works with all other data types).

```
DECLARE @SaleDate date
```

Query 10-41

We can select the variable to display its value, but when created as shown in Query 10-41, the initiated value is null. To give the variable a value, use the `SET` command, much like how we'd do it in an `UPDATE` statement (except you don't actually need the phrase `UPDATE`).

```
SET @SaleDate = '2021-01-14'
```

Query 10-42

Now, if the variable is selected, it will reflect the date that was just assigned to it. But in the spirit of everything we've learned so far, *why do something in two steps when you can accomplish the same thing in just one?* You can declare a variable and set its value in the same command if you place = **Value** immediately after the declaration.

```
DECLARE @Variable Name    Data Type = Value
```

Syntax 10-15

150

For example:

```
DECLARE @SaleDate date = '2021-01-14'
```
Query 10-43

You can even use a subquery to set the value of a variable.

```
DECLARE @SaleDate date = (SELECT MAX(PurchaseDate) FROM dbo.SampleTable)
```
Query 10-44

Going back to the start of this chapter, by using variables, you can set all the filter conditions equal to the variable, and then simply change the value of the variable as needed.

```
DECLARE @SaleDate date = '2021-01-14'

SELECT Columns
  FROM 1st Table
 WHERE SaleDate = @SaleDate
 UNION
SELECT Columns
  FROM 2nd Table
 WHERE SaleDate = @SaleDate
 UNION
SELECT Columns
  FROM 3rd Table
 WHERE SaleDate = @SaleDate
```
Syntax 10-16

This saves you the effort of changing the filters any time an update is needed. Changing the variable declaration line will affect all three statements below it, rather than having to change all three lines manually.

10.13 Temporary Tables

Sometimes, it's just not worth the effort to create a new table. You may need something that's similar in functionality to a table, but don't want to keep a copy of it in your database after you're finished; you'd just like it to go away after you close the program. This can be completed with a temporary table.

A temporary table can be created in the same way that regular tables are created (chapter 2.3 and chapter 3.6). The name of the temporary table must begin with a pound symbol, # (a.k.a. the hashtag, or a.k.a. the *octothorpe*). For temporary tables, you do not need to use the prefix *dbo*.

With a few exceptions, you can do just about anything with a temporary table that you can do with a regular table: selecting from them (Query 10-45), inserting into them, aggregating them, etc. Since the syntax doesn't change between regular tables and temporary tables, it would be superfluous to give many examples.

```
SELECT * FROM #TempTable
```

Query 10-45

There are two caveats with temporary tables. The first is that if the connection to the database is dropped or lost (such as if you close the query), the temporary table is dropped as well. As long as a connection is maintained, the temporary table will be retained (unless of course you choose to drop the table). The second caveat is that the temporary table is only visible within the connection that opened it. Every query file or editor that you have open is its own connection. If I open two different files within SSMS, I will have created two connections. A temporary table created within the first connection is not visible to the second connection.

If you would like temporary tables to be visible to all connections, use a double pound sign in front of the table name (e.g., ##TempTable) instead of just one.

10.14 Views

Suppose you have a lengthy, complex query that you run on a regular basis. Every time you wish to view the results of the query, you'll likely have to open the query file and run it. On top of this, if you wished to use the results of the query as part of another query, you would have to load the results into a table or use a large subquery, neither of which are an ideal solution. Each has their own pros and cons, but a good middle-ground solution is to use a *view*.

A view is a table/query hybrid. Like tables, rows and columns can be selected from a view using a select statement. Views can be aliased, used in joins, and used in many other operations that you would typically use a table for. Unlike tables, views don't actually store any data. A view is actually just a query pretending to be a table. Whenever you "select" from a view, you're actually executing the underlying query.

Going back to our hypothetical query, it would be advantageous to save it as a view. One advantage over inserting the results in a table is that the view will always pull the latest data from its source tables. Storing the results in a table will require updating if any of the source tables are updated. One of the disadvantages of views is that if the query normally takes a long time to execute, storing it in a view will not necessarily increase its performance.

The table below, *dbo.CityTemperature*, represents the highest temperature (in Celsius) per month over the course of seven months in a major city. I wish to use this data in Query 10-46.

dbo.CityTemperature	
LocalDate	**Temperature**
2020-01-01	0
2020-02-01	-3
2020-03-01	6
2020-04-01	12
2020-05-01	20
2020-06-01	25
2020-07-01	29

Table 10-43

```
SELECT LocalDate,
       Temperature,
       CASE WHEN Temperature <= 32 THEN 'Freezing cold'
            WHEN Temperature <= 50 THEN 'Very cold'
            WHEN Temperature <= 65 THEN 'Warming up'
            WHEN Temperature <= 75 THEN 'Warm'
            ELSE 'Hot'
        END AS TempDescription
  FROM dbo.CityTemperature
```

Query 10-46

The problem is that the query is set up for use in Fahrenheit. Without any adjustments, this query would say that 32° C is freezing cold, when in fact, it is about 90° F. There are a few ways to get the data and query to mesh properly. One way is to simply adjust 32° F, 50° F, 65° F, and 75° F in the query to their Celsius equivalents, but for sake of argument, let's say that those values cannot change. Another way is to adjust the query to replace every instance of **Temperature** with the Fahrenheit equivalent (since it will be reading in Celsius values from the table). This means replacing each with (Temperature * 9.0/5.0) + 32. While certainly doable, it may also make the code difficult to read.

```
SELECT LocalDate,
       (Temperature * 9.0/5.0) + 32 AS Temperature,
       CASE WHEN (Temperature * 9.0/5.0) + 32 <= 32 THEN 'Freezing cold'
            WHEN (Temperature * 9.0/5.0) + 32 <= 50 THEN 'Very cold'
            WHEN (Temperature * 9.0/5.0) + 32 <= 65 THEN 'Warming up'
            WHEN (Temperature * 9.0/5.0) + 32 <= 75 THEN 'Warm'
            ELSE 'Hot'
         END AS TempDescription
  FROM dbo.CityTemperature
```

Query 10-47

Another way is to use a subquery or CTE to first convert all of the temperatures to Fahrenheit, alias it as **Temperature**, and then using the rest of the query verbatim.

```
SELECT LocalDate,
       Temperature,
       CASE WHEN Temperature <= 32 THEN 'Freezing cold'
            WHEN Temperature <= 50 THEN 'Very cold'
            WHEN Temperature <= 65 THEN 'Warming up'
            WHEN Temperature <= 75 THEN 'Warm'
            ELSE 'Hot'
         END AS TempDescription
  FROM (
        SELECT LocalDate,
               (Temperature * 9.0/5.0) + 32 AS Temperature
          FROM dbo.CityTemperature
       ) AS T
```

Query 10-48

This method is better, since very little code needs to be changed. But ultimately, it is more complex than is has to be. The easiest method would be to replace the subquery in Query 10-48 with a view that performs the same calculation. This will allow us to retain the simplicity of Query 10-46, without sacrificing any functionality.

```
CREATE VIEW View Name
       AS Query
```

Syntax 10-17

Views are typically named as *dbo.V_Name*, and are stored in the "Views" folder in the database, rather than the "Tables" folder. This is done to help differentiate them from regular tables. To create the view, we simply replace *query* in Syntax 10-17 with the subquery, and we will choose the name *dbo.V_CityTemperature_Fahrenheit*.

```
CREATE VIEW dbo.V_CityTemperature_Fahrenheit
       AS SELECT LocalDate,
                 (Temperature * 9.0/5.0) + 32 AS Temperature
            FROM dbo.CityTemperature
```

Query 10-49

After executing, the view will be created. If we select the data from the view, we will see the Fahrenheit equivalents of the temperatures.

dbo.V_CityTemperature_Fahrenheit	
LocalDate	**Temperature**
2020-01-01	32.000000
2020-02-01	26.600000
2020-03-01	42.800000
2020-04-01	53.600000
2020-05-01	68.000000
2020-06-01	77.000000
2020-07-01	84.200000

Table 10-44

The temperatures having six decimal places is merely a side-effect of the calculation; they will have no affect on the query. Finally, we can replace *dbo.CityTemperature* in Query 10-46 with *dbo.V_CityTemperature_Fahrenheit*.

```
SELECT LocalDate,
       Temperature,
       CASE WHEN Temperature <= 32 THEN 'Freezing cold'
            WHEN Temperature <= 50 THEN 'Very cold'
            WHEN Temperature <= 65 THEN 'Warming up'
            WHEN Temperature <= 75 THEN 'Warm'
            ELSE 'Hot'
          END AS TempDescription
  FROM dbo.V_CityTemperature_Fahrenheit
```

Query 10-50

Query Results		
LocalDate	**Temperature**	**TempDescription**
2020-01-01	32.000000	Freezing cold
2020-02-01	26.600000	Freezing cold
2020-03-01	42.800000	Very cold
2020-04-01	53.600000	Warming up
2020-05-01	68.000000	Warm
2020-06-01	77.000000	Hot
2020-07-01	84.200000	Hot

Table 10-45

Views can be dropped in a similar manner to dropping tables.

```
DROP VIEW View Name
```

Syntax 10-18

11 Appendix A: Indexes

11.1 What is an Index?

An index is a way of structuring data such that queries that retrieve data perform much faster. Consider the table below, where each row contains a random word.

dbo.ClusteredIndexTest
RandomWord
Guess
Three
Green
Stoop
Zip
Equable
Blade
Calculate
Title
Chair
Home
Loose
Chair
Bite
Open
Wheel

Table 11-1

If we searched for the word "chair," SQL would have to scan every row of *dbo.ClusteredIndexTest* to see if the value for **RandomWord** was equal to it. If they were equal, SQL would add the row to the result set and move onto the next row. If they were not equal, SQL would skip that particular row and move onto the next row. In this case, only the 10th and 13th rows will be returned in the results.

If the size of the table is small, then searching through all of the values won't take long. But if the table has millions of rows or more, searches may take longer. By creating an index, the performance of this same query can be drastically increased. In some cases, having an index can be the difference between a query finishing quickly, and a query taking so long that you get fed up and cancel it.

11.2 Clustered Indexes

11.2.1 Dictionary Analogy

To understand the crux of a clustered index, imagine that you have a copy of the Merriam-Webster dictionary and wanted to search for the definition of the word "bathypelagic." Why might it be inefficient to flip to random pages in different portions of the dictionary, hoping to find the word? For starters, dictionaries are in alphabetical order. Since bathypelagic starts with a B, it will probably be somewhere in the first 20% of the pages, meaning that 80% of the entire dictionary can be skipped.

From there, the search needs to get a little more fine-tuned. Assume that the first 20% of the dictionary included the chapters for A, B, C, and D. At a glance (even without reading the words in their entirety), it's easy to tell if the words on the page start with a B or not. And if they don't, the entire chapter can be skipped. All that remains in the search is the B chapter.

On the top of each page of a dictionary, there are guide words. These represent the first and last words that appear on that page and provide a further refinement in searching. If the chosen word falls outside of the range of the guide words alphabetically, the entire page can be skipped. Eventually, you'll reach the page where the word falls *inside* the range of the guide words, at which point a word-by-word search will be needed. In total, since the dictionary is in alphabetical order, 99% of the searching was done in a few steps, and there was a minimum of line-by-line searching. This is the same concept behind a clustered index.

And in case you were wondering, bathypelagic means relating to or living between 2,000 and 12,000 feet under the ocean's surface.

11.2.2   Operation and Function

Clustered indexes are built on one or more columns that are selected at the time of creation. The columns are typically the ones that will be searched often. In *dbo.ClusteredIndexTest*, **RandomWord** was searched through for a particular value, so that column will be indexed.

When creating the index, SQL will sort the data based on the chosen column. This is different than using ORDER BY, which only temporarily sorts the data when displaying the results. A clustered index physically alters the arrangement of the original data in the table.

dbo.ClusteredIndexTest
RandomWord
Bite
Blade
Calculate
Chair
Chair
Equable
Green
Guess
Home
Loose
Open
Stoop
Three
Title
Wheel
Zip

Table 11-2

SQL will then create a balanced-tree or "B-Tree" structure:

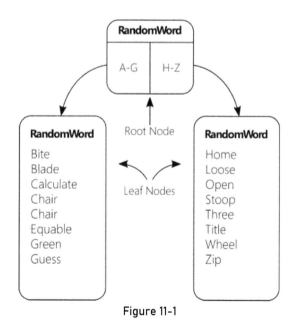

Figure 11-1

SQL will organize the data into groups based on their values. Any values that start with an A through a G are organized into one group (called a leaf node), and anything that starts with an H through a Z is organized into another leaf node. Other data types will be handled in a similar manner. At this point, the clustered index has been created.

When searching for a value with the help of a clustered index, SQL will look at the left-most character of the value that is being searched for. Returning back to the top of the chapter, we were searching for "chair," making the first letter "c." According to the root node at the top, anything that starts with a character between A and G was placed in the leaf node on the left. Because of this tree structure, we've immediately eliminated 50% of all of the data that SQL would have otherwise needed to search through.

Furthermore, since the data inside the leaf nodes are ordered alphabetically, any repeating values will be next to each other. While searching for "chair," SQL will find the two instances of the word next to each other, and eventually reach "equable." Since the data is alphabetical, "chair" can never appear after "equable," so SQL knows that it can stop searching. If the data were not in alphabetical order, SQL would not know if there were any more instances after the copy that it had found, so it would need to continue searching.

How SQL Server chooses to create/optimize the index will depend on the data itself, and how many rows are contained within the table. Having many more rows will increase the depth of the index, or how many nodes there are. In Figure 11-1, we only have a depth of one, meaning one node. Larger tables may have a depth of two or three, meaning that there are intermediate nodes between the root node and leaf nodes.

Clustered indexes do take up some space, but no new data is being introduced into the table, nor is any data being copied from it. Think of it like this, the pages in a book can be rearranged in any order, but the number of pages never increases or decreases. Very little additional space is needed to create a clustered index, which is a useful consideration for databases short on space.

11.2.3   Creating and Deleting a Clustered Index

A clustered index can be created easily. In the following syntax, ***columns*** is a comma separated list of the columns that will be indexed. If, for example, you have table of customer information, and typically search for customers based on account number, then the account number column should be indexed. If you typically search based on both account number *and* name, then both the account number and name columns should be indexed.

```
CREATE CLUSTERED INDEX Index Name ON Table
(
        Columns
)
```

Syntax 11-1

The position of the columns in the query is important when creating a clustered index. An index created on account number first and then name is not the same as an index created on name first and then account number. If a table is indexed on account number first, and then name second, but you search through the table by name only, you will not reap the rewards of having an index. The index is optimized to search for account number first. More information about multi-column indexes can be found in chapter 11.4.

Indexes can be dropped using the following syntax.

```
DROP INDEX Index Name ON Table
```

Syntax 11-2

11.3 Non-Clustered Indexes
11.3.1 Textbook Analogy
Non-clustered indexes work differently than clustered indexes, so we'll have to switch up the analogy a bit. Instead of a dictionary, we'll assume that we have a textbook. A textbook is not ordered alphabetically. And if we did order a textbook alphabetically, it would be a jumbled, incoherent mess. But despite this fact, it is still possible to find information in a textbook rather easily.

If we wanted to find every instance of the word "momentum" in a physics textbook, we would reference the index in the back of the book. The index will tell us which pages make use of the word "momentum."

In a broad sense, what is the index of a book? The index takes a copy all of the distinct or important words from the book, orders them alphabetically for easy lookups, and then gives the locations where the values appear in the original text. The index in the back of the book doesn't actually change the order of the original text, it only gives the locations of each instance of each word.

11.3.2 Operation and Function

A non-clustered index operates like the index of a book; it makes a copy of the data, organizes the *copy* into a clustered index, and in the clustered index, gives the location(s) within the original data where the particular value is found. Because the copy is being organized, the original data remains untouched.

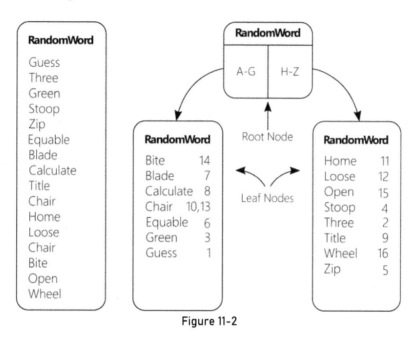

Figure 11-2

If we now search for "chair," instead of searching through the original table, SQL will begin searching through the B-tree made from the copy of the data. Once it finds "chair," it will see that the word appears on the 10th and 13th rows of the original table. SQL will then know exactly where to go to find the data it's looking for.

11.3.3 Creating and Deleting a Non-Clustered Index

A non-clustered index is created in much the same way as a clustered index. The syntax differs only in the word NONCLUSTERED versus CLUSTERED.

```
CREATE NONCLUSTERED INDEX Index Name ON Table
(
        Columns
)
```

Syntax 11-3

A non-clustered index can be dropped in the same manner as a clustered index, by using Syntax 11-2.

11.4 Clustered vs Non-Clustered Indexes

What else makes a non-clustered index different compared to a clustered index? As I explained earlier, a clustered index does not take up much space. As a test, I created a table of 5,000,000 strings of random numbers and letters. The table took up approximately 100 MB, but the clustered index only took up 0.2 MB.

With a non-clustered index, SQL must store a copy of the values in the indexed column, along with the pointers to the original data where those values appear, which takes up additional space. The size of the non-clustered index on this table was approximately 100 MB.

Because clustered indexes physically alter the original data, there cannot be two different clustered indexes created on the same table, as it is impossible to sort a single set of data in two different ways (to clarify, there can be more than one column per index, but not more than one clustered index per table). Earlier, I mentioned an example of a table indexed by account number first, and then name, and how searching by name only would not yield any benefit. With this in mind, it is important to choose a clustered index such that it closely matches how searches will be performed. If the vast majority of your searches will always be on the same column(s), it's wise to create a clustered index based on those columns.

A non-clustered index does not alter the original data, it only creates and alters the copies, so it is possible to have more than one non-clustered index on the same table. Therefore, if some of your searches rely on account number only, and some of your searches rely on name only, it would be beneficial to create two non-clustered indexes; one on each column.

Non-clustered indexes have another significant difference: the option to have *included columns*. Picture a table of people with five columns, and an accompanying non-clustered index based on the name.

dbo.IncludedColumnsTest						Non-Clustered Index	
PersonName	DateOfBirth	Height	Weight	BirthPlace		PersonName	Location
Noel Villarreal	1978-04-10	5' 10"	185	UK		Frederic Wong	Row 5
Joseph Wilson	1992-08-27	4' 9"	130	USA		Heather Mclean	Row 3
Heather Mclean	1989-03-23	5' 2"	150	USA		Joseph Wilson	Row 2
Margarito Tran	1982-12-31	6' 3"	210	Brazil		Margarito Tran	Row 4
Frederic Wong	1982-08-06	5' 5"	155	China		Noel Villarreal	Row 1

Table 11-3 and Table 11-4

If you wrote a query to find the birthdate of someone by searching for their name (i.e., `SELECT DateOfBirth FROM dbo.IncludedColumnsTest WHERE PersonName = ...`), SQL would look that name up in the non-clustered index, find out where in the original data that value was found, go to said row in the original table, and then pull the birthdate. We can skip two of these steps by having **DateOfBirth** as an "included" column. When a non-clustered index is created with an included column, a copy of the values from that column will be added to the index.

dbo.IncludedColumnsTest						Non-Clustered Index		
PersonName	DateOfBirth	Height	Weight	BirthPlace		PersonName	DateOfBirth	Location
Noel Villarreal	1978-04-10	5' 10"	185	UK		Frederic Wong	1982-08-06	Row 5
Joseph Wilson	1992-08-27	4' 9"	130	USA		Heather Mclean	1989-03-23	Row 3
Heather Mclean	1989-03-23	5' 2"	150	USA		Joseph Wilson	1992-08-27	Row 2
Margarito Tran	1982-12-31	6' 3"	210	Brazil		Margarito Tran	1982-12-31	Row 4
Frederic Wong	1982-08-06	5' 5"	155	China		Noel Villarreal	1978-04-10	Row 1

Table 11-5 and Table 11-6

Now, when searching for the birth date based on name, SQL no longer has to even reference the original table. We included a copy of **DateOfBirth** in the index, meaning that instead of doing the lookup to the original table based on **PersonName**, we just use the copy of **DateOfBirth** stored in the index.

Syntax 11-4 shows how to create a non-clustered index with included columns. The columns that are indexed cannot be used as included columns.

```
CREATE NONCLUSTERED INDEX Index Name ON Table
(
        Indexed Columns
)
INCLUDE
(
        Included Columns
)
```

Syntax 11-4

Note that having included columns is not the same thing as having a non-clustered index that is built on two or more columns. Indexed columns are part of the B-tree structure, included columns are just tacked on at the end. As a rule of thumb, if it's in your WHERE clause, it should be one of the indexed columns. If it's in the columns of your SELECT list, it should be an included column.

12 Appendix B: Selected Functions
12.1 Aggregate
AVG

Description:

Computes the average of the values within a group or partition.

Syntax:

AVG (*Column*)

Example:

dbo.AVG_Example
TestValues
1
5
3
8
3

```
SELECT AVG(TestValues) AS AVG_Results FROM dbo.AVG_Example
```

Query Results
AVG_Results
4

Notes:

If the column being averaged has an integer data type, and the average value is not an integer (i.e., the average of four and five), the result will be rounded *towards* zero. The average value of four and five (4.5) will be rounded to four. The average value of -4 and -5 (-4.5) will be rounded to -4.

COUNT

Description:
Counts the number of the values within a group or partition.

Syntax:
COUNT(*), COUNT(**Column**), or COUNT(DISTINCT **Column**)

Example:

dbo.COUNT_Example
TestValues
1
5
3
8
3

```
SELECT COUNT(TestValues) AS COUNT_Results FROM dbo.COUNT_Example
```

Query Results
COUNT_Results
5

Notes:
See chapter 5.1 for more information regarding the different options for the COUNT function.

GROUPING

Description:
Distinguishes nulls in data from nulls as a result of aggregation.

Syntax:
GROUPING(***Column***)

Example:

dbo.GROUPING_Example	
PurchaseDate	**PurchasePrice**
2020-07-22	43.13
NULL	12.58
2020-07-25	54.09
2020-07-25	37.18
NULL	78.91
2020-07-29	62.34

```
  SELECT PurchaseDate,
         GROUPING(PurchaseDate) AS GROUPING_Results,
         SUM(PurchasePrice) AS Sum_Purchases
    FROM dbo.GROUPING_Example
GROUP BY ROLLUP(PurchaseDate)
```

Query Results		
PurchaseDate	**GROUPING_Results**	**Sum_Purchases**
NULL	0	91.49
2020-07-22	0	43.13
2020-07-25	0	91.27
2020-07-29	0	62.34
NULL	1	288.23

Notes:
In the query results table, there are two instances of null values for **PurchaseDate**. One of them refers to the grouping of null entries in the **PurchaseDate** column, and the other refers to the entry automatically created by the ROLLUP clause; the $91.49 entry, and the $288.23 entry, respectively. We can distinguish these two rows from each other by the middle column, **GROUPING_Results**. A value of zero means that this particular row is *not* the results of a ROLLUP, CUBE, or GROUPING SETS aggregation. Similarly, a value of one means that the row *is* the result of a ROLLUP, CUBE, or GROUPING SETS aggregation.

MAX

Description:
Computes the maximum of the values within a group or partition.

Syntax:
MAX(*Column*)

Example:

dbo.MAX_Example
TestValues
1
5
3
8
3

```
SELECT MAX(TestValues) AS MAX_Results FROM dbo.MAX_Example
```

Query Results
MAX_Results
8

MIN

Description:
Computes the minimum of the values within a group or partition.

Syntax:
MIN(*Column*)

Example:

dbo.MIN_Example
TestValues
1
5
3
8
3

```
SELECT MIN(TestValues) AS MIN_Results FROM dbo.MIN_Example
```

Query Results
MIN_Results
1

STDEV

Description:
Computes the standard deviation of the values within a group or partition.

Syntax:
STDEV (*Column*)

Example:

dbo.STDEV_Example
TestValues
1
5
3
8
3

```
SELECT STDEV(TestValues) AS STDEV_Results FROM dbo.STDEV_Example
```

Query Results
STDEV_Results
2.64575131106459

SUM

Description:
Computes the sum of the values within a group or partition.

Syntax:
SUM (*Column*)

Example:

dbo.SUM_Example
TestValues
1
5
3
8
3

```
SELECT SUM(TestValues) AS SUM_Results FROM dbo.SUM_Example
```

Query Results
SUM_Results
20

VAR

Description:
Computes the variance of the values within a group or partition.

Syntax:
VAR(*Column*)

Example:

dbo.VAR_Example
TestValues
1
5
3
8
3

```
SELECT VAR(TestValues) AS VAR_Results FROM dbo.VAR_Example
```

Query Results
VAR_Results
7

12.2 Analytical

CUME_DIST

Description:

Computes the portion (normalized to 100% = 1.0) of rows with values less than or equal to those of the current row. The median is by definition the 50th percentile (or 0.5, meaning 50% of all other values are less than or equal to it).

Syntax:

CUME_DIST() OVER (ORDER BY **Column**)

Example:

dbo.CUME_DIST_Example
TestValues
1
2
2
4
7

```
SELECT TestValues, CUME_DIST() OVER (ORDER BY TestValues) AS CUME_DIST_Results
  FROM dbo.CUME_DIST_Example
```

Query Results	
TestValues	**CUME_DIST_Results**
1	0.2
2	0.6
2	0.6
4	0.8
7	1

Description:

Retrieves the data from an earlier row within the same dataset (without joining a table to itself). The row which is selected will depend on how the data is sorted (within the ORDER BY clause), and the *offset* value, i.e., how many rows prior to the current row.

Syntax:

LAG(**Column, Offset**) OVER (ORDER BY **Column**)

Example:

dbo.LAG_Example
TestValues
2021-01-04
2021-01-10
2021-01-15
2021-01-30
2021-02-05

```
SELECT TestValues, LAG(TestValues, 1) OVER (ORDER BY TestValues) AS LAG_Results
  FROM dbo.LAG_Example
```

Query Results	
TestValues	**LAG_Results**
2021-01-04	NULL
2021-01-10	2021-01-04
2021-01-15	2021-01-10
2021-01-30	2021-01-15
2021-02-05	2021-01-30

Notes:

In the results above, the results of the LAG function are the dates that occur one row before the dates in **TestValues**. Since no date occurs before 2021-01-04, that field is null. There is a third optional parameter within the first set of parentheses which dictates what to default the value to if no prior value is found. Had I specified that the default value was 2021-01-01, the null field in the table above would have been that date.

Additionally, LAG supports partitioning, and is implemented in the same way you would for ROW_NUMBER, RANK, and DENSE_RANK.

```
LEAD
```

Description:
Retrieves the data from a later row within the same dataset (without joining a table to itself). The row which is selected will depend on how the data is sorted (within the ORDER BY clause), and the *offset* value, i.e., how many rows after the current row.

Syntax:
```
LEAD(Column, Offset) OVER (ORDER BY Column)
```

Example:

dbo.LEAD_Example
TestValues
2020-01-04
2020-01-10
2020-01-15
2020-01-30
2020-02-05

```
SELECT TestValues,
       LEAD(TestValues, 1) OVER (ORDER BY TestValues) AS LEAD_Results
  FROM dbo.LEAD_Example
```

Query Results	
TestValues	**LEAD_Results**
2021-01-04	2021-01-10
2021-01-10	2021-01-15
2021-01-15	2021-01-30
2021-01-30	2021-02-05
2021-02-05	NULL

Notes:
LEAD and LAG are merely opposite functions. LAG retrieves data from rows prior to the current row, and LEAD retrieves data from rows after the current row. LEAD also has the option for a default value.

Additionally, LEAD supports partitioning, and is implemented in the same way you would for ROW_NUMBER, RANK, and DENSE_RANK.

```
PERCENTILE_CONT
```

Description:

Computes the specified percentile (normalized to 100% = 1) of rows within a column. This function assumes a continuous distribution of values, so the computed value may not actually be found within the data.

Syntax:
```
PERCENTILE_CONT (Percentile)
   WITHIN GROUP (ORDER BY Column)
           OVER (PARTITION BY Column)
```


Example:

dbo.PERCENTILE_CONT_Example
TestValues
100000
60000
92000
74000
85000
57000

```
SELECT DISTINCT PERCENTILE_CONT (0.5)
                WITHIN GROUP (ORDER BY TestValues)
                    OVER () AS PERCENTILE_CONT_Results
 FROM dbo.PERCENTILE_CONT_Example
```

Query Results
PERCENTILE_CONT_Results
79500

Notes:

The PARTITION BY clause is not required, but due to the unusual nature of the syntax for PERCENTILE_CONT, I have included it. Notice that the result of the query is not a value that actually appears in the original data. This is the nature of the continuous percentile; it interprets where the percentile would fall if an exact match doesn't exist.

```
PERCENTILE_DISC
```

Description:

Computes the specified percentile (normalized to 100% = 1) of rows within a column. This function assumes a discrete distribution of values, so the computed value will be found within the data.

Syntax:
```
PERCENTILE_DISC (Percentile)
   WITHIN GROUP (ORDER BY Column)
           OVER (PARTITION BY Column)
```

Example:

dbo.PERCENTILE_DISC_Example
TestValues
100000
60000
92000
74000
85000
57000

```
SELECT DISTINCT PERCENTILE_DISC (0.5)
                WITHIN GROUP (ORDER BY TestValues)
                      OVER () AS PERCENTILE_DISC_Results
 FROM dbo.PERCENTILE_DISC_Example
```

Query Results
PERCENTILE_DISC_Results
74000

Notes:

The PARTITION BY clause is not required, but due to the unusual nature of the syntax for PERCENTILE_DISC, I have included it.

PERCENT_RANK

Description:
Computes the relative rank of a row compared to other rows within a column, normalized to highest rank = 1.

Syntax:
PERCENT_RANK() OVER (ORDER BY **Column**)

Example:

dbo.PERCENT_RANK_Example
TestValues
1
2
2
4
7

```
SELECT TestValues,
       PERCENT_RANK() OVER (ORDER BY TestValues) AS PERCENT_RANK_Results
  FROM dbo.PERCENT_RANK_Example
```

Query Results	
TestValues	**PERCENT_RANK_Results**
1	0
2	0.25
2	0.25
4	0.75
7	1

Notes:
The PERCENT_RANK is approximately equal to the following equation:

$$\text{Percent Rank} = \frac{\text{Row Rank} - 1}{\text{Count of Records} - 1}$$

In the table above, the value of four will also have a rank of four, and the total record count is five, making the equation:

$$\text{Percent Rank} = \frac{4 - 1}{5 - 1} = \frac{3}{4} = 0.75$$

Additionally, PERCENT_RANK supports partitioning, and is implemented in the same way you would for ROW_NUMBER, RANK, and DENSE_RANK. With regards to the calculation, the Row Rank and Count of Records would all be relative to the partition.

12.3 Conversion
CAST

Description:
Converts a value from one data type to another data type.

Syntax:
CAST(*Value* AS *Data Type*)

Example:
```
SELECT CAST('2020-03-23 17:40:39.317' AS DATE) AS CAST_Results
```

Query Results
CAST_Results
2020-03-23

Notes:
Some of (but not all of) the available data types are given in chapter 2.2.

CONVERT

Description:
Converts a value from one data type to another data type. Optionally allows for an input/output style.

Syntax:
CONVERT(*Data Type*, *Value*, *Style*)

Example:
```
SELECT CONVERT(DATE, '23.03.2020', 104) AS CONVERT_Results
```

Query Results
CONVERT_Results
2020-03-23

Notes:
The *style* refers to the formatting of the input when converting to a date. When converting to character data, it refers to the formatting of the output. Using style code 104 in the example above informs SQL that the input date is of the form *DD.MM.YYYY*. A list of style codes can be found in Microsoft's T-SQL documentation online.

A good place to start would be here:
https://docs.microsoft.com/en-us/sql/t-sql/functions/cast-and-convert-transact-sql

12.4 Date and Time
DATEADD

Description:
Adds a specified number of dateparts (increments; days, weeks, months, etc.) to a date.

Syntax:
DATEADD(***Datepart, Number, Date***)

Example:
```
SELECT DATEADD(WEEK, 3, '2021-01-08') AS DATEADD_Results
```

Query Results
DATEADD_Results
2020-01-29

Notes:
A valid ***datepart*** is necessary (shown below). To add to a date, a positive number must be entered for the second parameter. To subtract from a date, a negative number must be entered.

In instances such as DATEADD(MONTH, 1, '2021-01-31'), since February does not have 31 days, the query will return the maximum allowable date for February, February 28th, 2021 (or 29th if it is a leap year). It will never return results such as February 31st, 2021.

Valid SQL dateparts (both the full-length and abbreviations are acceptable):

Full-length	Abbreviation
Year	yy, yyyy
Quarter	qq, q
Month	mm, m
Dayofyear	dy, d
Day	dd, d
Week	wk, ww
Weekday	dw, w
Hour	hh
Minute	mi, n
Second	ss, s
Millisecond	ms
Microsecond	msc
Nanosecond	ns

DATEDIFF

Description:
Calculates the difference between two dates in units of **datepart**.

Syntax:
DATEDIFF(**Datepart, Start Date, End Date**)

Example:
To calculate the difference in days between March 8th, 2020 and July 2nd, 2020:

```
SELECT DATEDIFF(DAY, '2020-03-08', '2020-07-02') AS DATEDIFF_Results
```

Query Results
DATEDIFF_Results
116

Notes:
A valid datepart is necessary. The function will return a positive value if the start date occurs prior to the end date, negative otherwise. All results are whole numbers. For example, May 31st, 2020 to June 1st, 2020 is only one day, but since May is the 5th month, and June is the 6th month, the difference between these two dates in terms of months is one.

DATEFROMPARTS

Description:
Constructs a date value from the specified year, month, and day.

Syntax:
DATEFROMPARTS(*Year, Month, Day*)

Example:
```
SELECT DATEFROMPARTS(2021, 2, 11) AS DATEFROMPARTS_Results
```

Query Results
DATEFROMPARTS_Results
2021-02-11

Notes:
Year, month, and day must all be integer values. Month names (January, February, etc.) cannot be given as the month parameter.

DATENAME

Description:
Returns the name of the chosen datepart of the specified date.

Syntax:
DATENAME(*Datepart, Date*)

Example:
```
SELECT DATENAME(Weekday, '2020-11-07') AS DATENAME_Results
```

Query Results
DATENAME_Results
Saturday

Notes:
Where applicable, it will return the name of the datepart, rather than a number. I.e., using DATENAME(MONTH, *date*) will return the name of the month, not the number of the month. The same concept applies to weekdays. Using Weekday or dw as the datepart will return the name of the day (Monday, Tuesday, etc.) instead of the number of the day with respect to a seven-day week.

DATEPART

Description:
Returns the number of the chosen datepart of the date passed to the function.

Syntax:
DATEPART(*Datepart, Date*)

Example:
```
SELECT DATEPART(Weekday, '2020-11-07') AS DATEPART_Results
```

Query Results
DATEPART_Results
7

Notes:
Unlike DATENAME, DATEPART will always return the *number* of the datepart. Specifying MONTH as the datepart will return the number of the month, 1-12, not the name. Similarly, using Weekday as the datepart will return the number of the weekday with respect to a seven-day week.

DAY

Description:
Returns the day of the month of the specified date.

Syntax:
DAY(*Date*)

Example:
```
SELECT DAY('2020-05-25') AS DAY_Results
```

Query Results
DAY_Results
25

Notes:
The DAY function will return the same value as DATEPART(DAY, *Date*).

EOMONTH

Description:
Returns a date corresponding to the last day of the month specified.

Syntax:
EOMONTH(*Date, Month Offset*)

Example:

```
SELECT EOMONTH('2020-09-13') AS EOMONTH_Results
SELECT EOMONTH('2020-09-13', 1) AS EOMONTH_Results
SELECT EOMONTH('2020-09-13', -1) AS EOMONTH_Results
```

Query Results
EOMONTH_Results
2020-09-30

Query Results
EOMONTH_Results
2020-10-31

Query Results
EOMONTH_Results
2020-08-31

Notes:
Month offset is optional. It specifies the number of months, positive or negative, that the date will be offset by. A value of one will return the end of the next month. A value of negative one will return the end of the previous month.

GETDATE

Description:
Returns the current date and time.

Syntax:
GETDATE()

Example:

```
SELECT GETDATE() AS GETDATE_Results
```

Query Results
GETDATE_Results
2020-03-18 12:18:26.250

ISDATE

Description:
Returns a value of one if the specified expression is a valid date, time, or datetime. Otherwise, it returns a value of zero.

Syntax:
ISDATE(**_Expression_**)

Example:

```
SELECT ISDATE('2020-06-25') AS ISDATE_Results
SELECT ISDATE(5) AS ISDATE_Results
```

Query Results
ISDATE_Results
1

Query Results
ISDATE_Results
0

```
MONTH
```

Description:
Returns the month of the specified date.

Syntax:
```
MONTH(Date)
```

Example:
```
SELECT MONTH('2020-05-25') AS MONTH_Results
```

Query Results
MONTH_Results
5

Notes:
The MONTH function will return the same value as DATEPART(MONTH, *Date*).

```
YEAR
```

Description:
Returns the year of the specified date.

Syntax:
```
YEAR(Date)
```

Example:
```
SELECT YEAR('2020-05-25') AS YEAR_Results
```

Query Results
YEAR_Results
2020

Notes:
The YEAR function will return the same value as DATEPART(YEAR, *Date*).

12.5 Mathematical

ABS

Description:

Returns the absolute value of the parameter.

Syntax:

ABS(**Number**)

Example:

```
SELECT ABS(-5) AS ABS_Results
```

Query Results
ABS_Results
5

ACOS

Description:

Returns the arccosine of the parameter in radians.

Syntax:

ACOS(**Number**)

Example:

```
SELECT ACOS(-1) AS ACOS_Results
```

Query Results
ACOS_Results
3.14159265358979

ASIN

Description:

Returns the arcsine of the parameter in radians.

Syntax:

ASIN(**Number**)

Example:

```
SELECT ASIN(1) AS ASIN_Results
```

Query Results
ASIN_Results
1.5707963267949

ATAN

Description:
Returns the arctangent of the parameter in radians.

Syntax:
ATAN(**Number**)

Example:

```
SELECT ATAN(1) AS ATAN_Results
```

Query Results
ATAN_Results
0.78539816339744

CEILING

Description:
Returns the smallest integer greater than or equal to the parameter.

Syntax:
CEILING(**Number**)

Example:

```
SELECT CEILING(3.7) AS CEILING_Results
```

Query Results
CEILING_Results
4

COS

Description:
Returns the cosine of the parameter (parameter given in radians).

Syntax:
COS(**Number**)

Example:

```
SELECT COS(0) AS COS_Results
```

Query Results
COS_Results
1

COT

Description:
Returns the cotangent of the parameter in radians.

Syntax:
COT (**Number**)

Example:

```
SELECT COT(3.14159265358979/4) AS COT_Results
```

Query Results
COT_Results
1

DEGREES

Description:
Returns the parameter converted to degrees (parameter given in radian).

Syntax:
DEGREES (**Number**)

Example:

```
SELECT DEGREES(1.0) AS DEGREES_Results
```

Query Results
DEGREES_Results
57.295779513082322865

EXP

Description:
Returns the value of the constant **e** raised to the power of the parameter.

Syntax:
EXP (**Number**)

Example:

```
SELECT EXP(1) AS EXP_Results
```

Query Results
EXP_Results
2.71828182845905

```
FLOOR
```

Description:
Returns the largest integer less than or equal to the parameter.

Syntax:
```
FLOOR(Number)
```

Example:
```
SELECT FLOOR(4.3) AS FLOOR_Results
```

Query Results
FLOOR_Results
4

```
LOG
```

Description:
Returns the logarithm of the parameter with the given base.

Syntax:
```
LOG(Number, Base)
```

Example:
```
SELECT LOG(1000, 10) AS LOG_Results
SELECT LOG(7.38905609893065) AS LOG_Results
```

Query Results
LOG_Results
3

Query Results
LOG_Results
2

Notes:
Base is optional. If it is not specified, it will default to the constant **e**, making it a natural logarithm.

LOG10

Description:
Returns the base-10 logarithm of the parameter.

Syntax:
LOG10 (**Number**)

Example:
```
SELECT LOG10(10000) AS LOG10_Results
```

Query Results
LOG10_Results
4

PI

Description:
Returns the value of pi.

Syntax:
PI()

Example:
```
SELECT PI() AS PI_Results
```

Query Results
PI_Results
3.14159265358979

POWER

Description:
Returns the value of first parameter raised to the power of the exponent.

Syntax:
POWER(**Number, Exponent**)

Example:
```
SELECT POWER(2, 3) AS POWER_Results
```

Query Results
POWER_Results
8

RADIANS

Description:
Returns the parameter converted to radians (parameter given in degrees).

Syntax:
RADIANS (*Number*)

Example:
```
SELECT RADIANS(180.0) AS RADIANS_Results
```

Query Results
RADIANS_Results
3.1415926535897933116

RAND

Description:
Returns a random number between (but not including) zero and one.

Syntax:
RAND()

Example:
```
SELECT RAND() AS RAND_Results
```

Query Results
RAND_Results
0.100505471175005

ROUND

Description:
Returns the parameter, rounded to a desired precision.

Syntax:
ROUND(**Number, Precision**)

Example:
```
SELECT ROUND(24.16, 1) AS ROUND_Results
SELECT ROUND(24.16, 0) AS ROUND_Results
SELECT ROUND(24.16, -1) AS ROUND_Results
```

Query Results
ROUND_Results
24.20

Query Results
ROUND_Results
24.00

Query Results
ROUND_Results
20.00

Notes:
Positive values for the **precision** will round the numbers to the right of the decimal point, and negative values will round to the left of the decimal point. The number of decimal places for both the input and output values will be the same.

SIGN

Description:
Returns the sign of the parameter as positive (+1), negative (-1) or neither (0).

Syntax:
SIGN(**Number**)

Example:
```
SELECT SIGN(-6) AS SIGN_Results
```

Query Results
SIGN_Results
-1

SIN

Description:
Returns the sine of the parameter (parameter given in radians).

Syntax:
SIN(**Number**)

Example:
```
SELECT SIN(1.5707963267949) AS SIN_Results
```

Query Results
SIN_Results
1

SQRT

Description:
Returns the square root of the parameter (does not work with negative numbers).

Syntax:
SQRT(**Number**)

Example:
```
SELECT SQRT(169) AS SQRT_Results
```

Query Results
SQRT_Results
13

SQUARE

Description:
Returns the square of the parameter.

Syntax:
SQUARE (*Number*)

Example:
```
SELECT SQUARE(13) AS SQUARE_Results
```

Query Results
SQUARE_Results
169

Notes:
The SQUARE function will return the same value as POWER(*Number*, 2).

TAN

Description:
Returns the tangent of the parameter (parameter given in radians).

Syntax:
TAN (*Number*)

Example:
```
SELECT TAN(3.14159265358979/4) AS TAN_Results
```

Query Results
TAN_Results
1

12.6 String

ASCII

Description:
Returns the ASCII code value for the leftmost character of the parameter.

Syntax:
ASCII(*String*)

Example:

```
SELECT ASCII('ABC') AS ASCII_Results
```

Query Results
ASCII_Results
65

CHAR

Description:
Returns the character corresponding to the ASCII code (the parameter).

Syntax:
CHAR(*Integer*)

Example:

```
SELECT CHAR(65) AS CHAR_Results
```

Query Results
CHAR_Results
A

CHARINDEX

Description:
Returns the starting position of the specified expression within another expression, or zero if it is not found.

Syntax:
CHARINDEX(***Search For, Within, Starting Position***)

Example:

```
SELECT CHARINDEX('good', 'have a good day, and a good night')
     AS CHARINDEX_Results
SELECT CHARINDEX('good', 'have a good day, and a good night', 9)
     AS CHARINDEX_Results
```

Query Results
CHARINDEX_Results
8

Query Results
CHARINDEX_Results
24

Notes:
The ***starting position*** parameter is optional. If it is utilized, SQL will start its search at the position given. In the first example, "good" is found in the 8th position. Since ***starting position*** is not given, the search will start at position one (the beginning of the string). In the second example, SQL is instructed to start the search at position nine. The first instance of "good" found after the ninth position is at the 24th position.

CONCAT

Description:
Returns the concatenation of the supplied parameters. Parameters may be strings, other literals, or columns.

Syntax:
CONCAT(*1st Value, 2nd Value, ...*)

Example:

dbo.CONCAT_Example					
Color1	Color2	Color3	Color4	Color5	Color6
Red	Orange	Yellow	Green	Blue	Purple

```
SELECT CONCAT(Color1, ' ', Color2, ' ',
              Color3, ' ', Color4, ' ',
              Color5, ' ', Color6) AS CONCAT_Results
  FROM dbo.CONCAT_Example
```

Query Results
CONCAT_Results
Red Orange Yellow Green Blue Purple

CONCAT_WS

Description:
Returns the concatenation of the supplied parameters, each separated by the given character. Values for parameters may be strings, other literals, or columns.

Syntax:
CONCAT_WS(**Separator, 1st Value, 2nd Value, …**)

Example:

dbo.CONCAT_WS_Example					
Color1	Color2	Color3	Color4	Color5	Color6
Red	Orange	Yellow	Green	Blue	Purple

```
SELECT CONCAT_WS(' ', Color1, Color2,
                 Color3, Color4,
                 Color5, Color6) AS CONCAT_WS_Results
  FROM dbo.CONCAT_WS_Example
```

Query Results
CONCAT_WS_Results
Red Orange Yellow Green Blue Purple

FORMAT

Description:
Returns the parameter in the given style and (optional) cultural style.

Syntax:
FORMAT(***Expression, Style, Culture***)

Example:
```
SELECT FORMAT(CAST('2020-04-19' AS DATE), 'd', 'en-gb') AS Date_Results
SELECT FORMAT(1234567890, '(###) ###-####') AS PhoneNumber_Results
SELECT FORMAT(18.91, 'c', 'de-de') AS Currency_Results
```

Query Results
Date_Results
19/04/2020

Query Results
PhoneNumber_Results
(123) 456-7890

Query Results
Currency_Results
18,91 €

Notes:
When using a cultural style, you must use a standard style format, and likewise, when using a custom format, you cannot use a cultural style. In the first query, 2020-04-19 is formatted the way that **d**ates are displayed in Great Britain. An alternative to using a standard format string and cultural style is to replace both with the custom style 'dd/MM/yyyy'. Note that these are *not* the same as the datepart values from several sections prior. The reason that 2020-04-19 is cast as a date is because the FORMAT function can accept many types of inputs, and would not be able to distinguish between a date and a string.

In the second query, 1234567890 is given a custom format in the style of a phone number, with each # representing a successive digit.

In the third query, 18.91 is formatted the way that **c**urrency is displayed in Germany.

A list of standard format strings and cultural styles can be found in Microsoft's T-SQL documentation online. A good place to start would be here:
https://docs.microsoft.com/en-us/sql/t-sql/functions/format-transact-sql

LEFT

Description:
Returns the first *n* characters of an expression, starting from the left side. Values for the **expression** may be string and character columns or literal strings.

Syntax:
LEFT(**Expression, N**)

Example:

```
SELECT LEFT('Left function test', 4) AS LEFT_Results
```

Query Results
LEFT_Results
Left

LEN

Description:
Returns the length of an expression. Values for the **expression** may be string and character columns or literal strings.

Syntax:
LEN(**Expression**)

Example:

```
SELECT LEN('Figure out this length') AS LEN_Results
```

Query Results
LEN_Results
22

```
LOWER
```

Description:

Returns the expression, with all characters converted to lower case. Values for the **expression** may be string and character columns or literal strings.

Syntax:
```
LOWER(Expression)
```

Example:

```
SELECT LOWER('This Will All Be Lower Case') AS LOWER_Results
```

Query Results
LOWER_Results
this will all be lower case

```
LTRIM
```

Description:

Returns the expression, with all whitespace characters trimmed off of the left side. Values for the **expression** may be string and character columns or literal strings.

Syntax:
```
LTRIM(Expression)
```

Example:

```
SELECT LTRIM('   No more left whitespaces') AS LTRIM_Results
```

Query Results
LTRIM_Results
No more left whitespaces

PATINDEX

Description:
Returns the starting position of the specified pattern within another expression, or zero if it is not found. Functions similarly to CHARINDEX, except searches for patterns instead of exact matches (chapter 4.6).

Syntax:
PATINDEX(**_Search For, Within_**)

Example:
```
SELECT PATINDEX('%pat[r-v]erns', 'looking for patterns') AS PATINDEX_Results
SELECT PATINDEX('%pat[bcd]gonias', 'looking for some patagonias') AS PATINDEX_Results
SELECT PATINDEX('%pat%gonias', 'found some patagonias') AS PATINDEX_Results
```

Query Results
PATINDEX_Results
13

Query Results
PATINDEX_Results
0

Query Results
PATINDEX_Results
12

Notes:
This function does not support a starting position parameter.

REPLACE

Description:
Returns the expression, but with all instances of a specified string value replaced by another string value. Values for the **expression** may be string and character columns or literal strings.

Syntax:
REPLACE(**Expression**, **Search For**, **Replace With**)

Example:

```
SELECT REPLACE('I dislike pizza', 'dislike', 'enjoy') AS REPLACE_Results
```

Query Results
REPLACE_Results
I enjoy pizza

REPLICATE

Description:
Returns the expression, repeated *n* times. Values for **expression** may be string columns or literal strings.

Syntax:
REPLICATE(**Expression**, **N**)

Example:

```
SELECT REPLICATE('Hello', 3) AS REPLICATE_Results
```

Query Results
REPLICATE_Results
HelloHelloHello

REVERSE

Description:
Returns the expression in reverse order. Values for the **expression** may be string and character columns or literal strings.

Syntax:
REVERSE(**Expression**)

Example:

```
SELECT REVERSE('Racecar') AS REVERSE_Results
```

Query Results
REVERSE_Results
racecaR

RIGHT

Description:
Returns the first **n** characters of an expression, starting from the right side. Values for the **expression** may be string and character columns or literal strings.

Syntax:
RIGHT(**Expression, N**)

Example:

```
SELECT RIGHT('Function test for Right', 5) AS RIGHT_Results
```

Query Results
RIGHT_Results
Right

```
RTRIM
```

Description:
Returns the expression, with all whitespace characters trimmed off of the right side. Values for the **expression** may be string and character columns or literal strings.

Syntax:
```
RTRIM(Expression)
```

Example:

```
SELECT RTRIM('No more right whitespaces   ') AS RTRIM_Results
```

Query Results
RTRIM_Results
No more right whitespaces

```
STRING_AGG
```

Description:
Combines multiple rows from a column into a single value, separated by a specified character.

Syntax:
```
STRING_AGG(Expression, Separator)
```

Example:

dbo.STRING_AGG_Example
RowOrder
First
Second
Third

```
SELECT STRING_AGG(RowOrder, ',') AS STRING_AGG_Results
  FROM dbo.STRING_AGG_Example
```

Query Results
STRING_AGG_Results
First,Second,Third

```
STRING_SPLIT
```

Description:
Separates a single row or value into multiple rows, delimited by a specified character. If no alias is applied, default column name for the results is "value."

Syntax:
```
STRING_AGG(Expression, Delimiter)
```

Example:

```
SELECT [value] AS STRING_SPLIT_Results
  FROM STRING_SPLIT('First,Second,Third', ',')
```

Query Results
STRING_SPLIT_Results
First
Second
Third

```
STUFF
```

Description:
Inserts a string inside another string, and optionally overwrites characters.

Syntax:
```
STUFF(Expression, Starting Position, Overwrite Length, Replace With)
```

Example:

```
SELECT STUFF('abcdefg', 3, 2, 'xyz') AS STUFF_Results
SELECT STUFF('abcdefg', 3, 0, 'xyz') AS STUFF_Results
```

Query Results
STUFF_Results
abxyzefg

Query Results
STUFF_Results
abxyzcdefg

Notes:
In the first example, the phrase xyz is inserted between the b and the c, and overwrites two letters in the process. In the second example, xyz is inserted between the b and the c, but doesn't overwrite any letters.

SUBSTRING

Description:
Returns a portion of an expression starting at a specified position, extending for a given length.

Syntax:
SUBSTRING(*Expression*, *Starting Position*, *Length*)

Example:

```
SELECT SUBSTRING('Laughter', 1, 5) AS SUBSTRING_Results
```

Query Results
SUBSTRING_Results
Laugh

TRANSLATE

Description:
Translates all specified characters within an expression to a different set of characters.

Syntax:
TRANSLATE(*Expression*, *Initial Set*, *Translated Set*)

Example:

```
SELECT TRANSLATE('abcde', 'bc', 'cd') AS TRANSLATE_Results
```

Query Results
TRANSLATE_Results
acdde

Notes:
Corresponding characters are replaced. All instances of the first character in the *initial set* are replaced with the first character in the *translated set*. The same applies for the remainder of the characters. Both character sets must be of the same length. TRANSLATE is *not* the equivalent of nested REPLACE functions. If nested REPLACE functions were used, the first pass would replace all "b"s with "c"s, yielding "accde." The second pass would replace all "c"s with "d"s, yielding the result "addde." In this instance, the second character was replaced twice; first to c, and then to d. TRANSLATE will only ever replace a character once.

```
TRIM
```

Description:
Returns the expression, with all leading and trailing whitespace characters removed.

Syntax:
```
TRIM(Characters FROM Expression)
```

Example:

```
SELECT TRIM('  No whitespace to the left or right  ') AS TRIM_Results
SELECT TRIM('., ' FROM ',  No characters on either side      .') AS TRIM_Results
```

Query Results
TRIM_Results
No whitespace to the left or right

Query Results
TRIM_Results
No characters on either side

Notes:
In the syntax for TRIM, **Characters** FROM is not required. If this portion is omitted, the function will trim leading and trailing spaces from the expression. If it is utilized, it will trim all of the characters within the first set of quotes from the expression. In the second example, there were commas, spaces, and periods on the left and right of the expression. In the quotes, the three characters supplied are a comma, a space, and a period. These characters were trimmed off of the ends of the expression, leaving only the bare expression remaining.

```
UPPER
```

Description:
Returns the expression, with all characters converted to upper case.

Syntax:
```
UPPER(Expression)
```

Example:

```
SELECT UPPER('This Will All Be Upper Case') AS UPPER_Results
```

Query Results
UPPER_Results
THIS WILL ALL BE UPPER CASE

12.7 System

COALESCE

Description:
Scans the expressions from left to right, and returns the first non-null expression. Expressions may be literals or columns.

Syntax:
COALESCE(*1st Expression, 2nd Expression, … Nth Expression*)

Example:

dbo.COALESCE_Example		
FirstName	MiddleName	LastName
NULL	Adam	Smith

```
SELECT COALESCE(FirstName, MiddleName, LastName) AS COALESCE_Results
  FROM dbo.COALESCE_Example
```

Query Results
COALESCE_Results
Adam

ISNULL

Description:
Returns the value of the first expression if it is not null. If it is, returns the value of the second expression.

Syntax:
ISNULL(*1st Expression, 2nd Expression*)

Example:

```
SELECT ISNULL('Hello', 'Goodbye') AS ISNULL_Results
SELECT ISNULL(NULL, 'Goodbye') AS ISNULL_Results
```

Query Results
ISNULL_Results
Hello

Query Results
ISNULL_Results
Goodbye

ISNUMERIC

Description:
Returns a value of one if the specified expression is a valid number. Otherwise, it returns a value of zero.

Syntax:
ISNUMERIC(***Expression***)

Example:

```
SELECT ISNUMERIC(10) AS ISNUMERIC_Results
SELECT ISNUMERIC('10') AS ISNUMERIC_Results
SELECT ISNUMERIC('10a') AS ISNUMERIC_Results
```

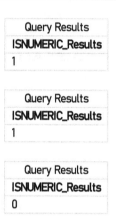

Notes:
ISNUMERIC will also return a value of one if ***expression*** is *capable* of being converted to a number. In the second example query, '10' is a string, but since it is capable of being converted to a number, ISNUMERIC will return one. In the third example query, '10a' cannot be converted to a number, therefore, ISNUMERIC will return zero.

```
NULLIF
```

Description:
Returns a null value if the two expressions are equal to each other, otherwise it returns the value of the first expression.

Syntax:
```
NULLIF(1st Expression, 2nd Expression)
```

Example:

```
SELECT NULLIF('a', 'a') AS NULLIF_Results
SELECT NULLIF('a', 'b') AS NULLIF_Results
```

Query Results
NULLIF_Results
NULL

Query Results
NULLIF_Results
a

13 Database Normalization

The design of your tables is just as, if not more, important than the queries used to retrieve data from them. Data that is not in "normal form" can be difficult to query against, update, and delete. Take for example the following table which describes customers of a cell phone company, along with what services they have on their account.

ID_Num	CustomerName	BillingAddress	Services	CreditScoreRange
1	Peter Walls	2805 West Side Avenue	Unlimited Texting, Unlimited Basic Data	500-600
2	Oliver Holden	1271 Browning Lane	Unlimited Texting, 10 GB High Speed Data	600-700
3	Sybil Baker	2482 Gore Street	50 GB International Data, Unlimited High-Speed Data, Smartwatch	700-800

dbo.MobileServices

Table 13-1

Suppose we wanted to find customers who had unlimited texting on their account. The obvious approach would be to add the condition WHERE Services = 'Unlimited Texting'. Or maybe not... Consider that all of the services on a customer's account are concatenated into a single comma delimited field. Using that simple WHERE clause approach would only work if Unlimited Texting was the *only* service on the account. But since these three accounts all have multiple services, it would be necessary to switch to a LIKE search instead, which is inherently slower. Similar issues will arise when you need to update or delete information.

The solution to these problems is to make sure that your data is in normal form.

13.1 First Normal Form (1NF)

To satisfy first normal form (1NF), no column should contain multiple values. Each service should be broken out into its own row.

		dbo.MobileServices		
ID_Num	CustomerName	BillingAddress	Services	CreditScoreRange
1	Peter Walls	2805 West Side Avenue	Unlimited Texting	500-600
1	Peter Walls	2805 West Side Avenue	Unlimited Basic Data	500-600
2	Oliver Holden	1271 Browning Lane	Unlimited Texting	600-700
2	Oliver Holden	1271 Browning Lane	10 GB High Speed Data	600-700
3	Sybil Baker	2482 Gore Street	50 GB International Data	700-800
3	Sybil Baker	2482 Gore Street	Unlimited High-Speed Data	700-800
3	Sybil Baker	2482 Gore Street	Smartwatch Access	700-800

Table 13-2

This form is much cleaner. Now if we want to do a search for a particular service, like Unlimited Texting, a simple WHERE clause would suffice. Likewise, UPDATE and DELETE statements will be much simpler. However, like we saw in chapter 8.4, in some ways, we've actually increased the amount of data in our table; not what we want. The solution is to separate Table 13-2 into a table of customer information (*dbo.MobileCustomers*), and a table of services (*dbo.MobileServices*). This will allow us to condense both tables.

	dbo.MobileCustomers		
ID_Num	CustomerName	BillingAddress	CreditScoreRange
1	Peter Walls	2805 West Side Avenue	500-600
2	Oliver Holden	1271 Browning Lane	600-700
3	Sybil Baker	2482 Gore Street	700-800

Table 13-3

	dbo.MobileServices
ID_Num	Services
1	Unlimited Texting
1	Unlimited Basic Data
2	Unlimited Texting
2	10 GB High Speed Data
3	50 GB International Data
3	Unlimited High-Speed Data
3	Smartwatch Access

Table 13-4

13.2 Second Normal Form (2NF)

Assume that the cell phone company wants to generate a report of sales. Every store reports their monthly sales numbers, and these values are inserted into a table. Stores are present in multiple states, and each state has several stores, all numbered one through N, where N is the number of stores. For example, New York may have stores, numbered one, two, three, ..., nine, ten. And Kentucky might have seven stores, numbered one, two, three, ..., six, seven. Therefore, we will need *both* the state *and* the store number to uniquely identify a store.

14 Index

15 Glossary

Aggregate function—A function applied to a column which calculates an aggregated value, such as the sum of all values within the column, or the count of values within a column.

Alias—A user-supplied name for a column. Used to replace the original name of the column, or to give a name to a calculated column which may not have one.

ALL—The clause used to check how a value compares against all values in another column. E.g., is the value for **PurchasePrice** greater than *all* the values in a different column? Will return true if it is greater than all of them.

ALTER—The clause used to modify a table or column after it has already been created.

BEGIN TRANSACTION—The statement used to indicate the beginning of a transaction.

BETWEEN—A clause used during filtering to indicate that a range of values may be searched.

B-Tree—A balanced tree. This is the organizational structure used when a clustered index is created.

CASE—A SQL function which will return different values based on multiple branches of logic. E.g., if some condition is true, return some value. If that first condition is not true, return a different value.

Column—A table object which stores an attribute about a row. If a table stores information about customers, each row represents one customer, and each column represents something about the customer, such as e-mail address.

Comment—Text found within the query that is not actually executed with the query. Is often used for making changes that can be easily reverted, or for notes.

COMMIT—The statement used to indicate that the changes made during a transaction can be committed to the database.

Common table expression—A method of creating a temporary table with aliases that can be referenced in a query without actually creating new table objects. Once the query is complete, the temporary tables are deleted.

CREATE—The clause used when creating a new object, such as a database or table.

CROSS APPLY—A subquery which will generate the cartesian join of the two tables.

CUBE—A clause that will cause SQL to create every possible permutation/combination of columns when calculating aggregate values.

Data type—The type of data that a column contains. A column of integers will have the INT data type. A column of dates will have the date data type, etc.

Database—A collection of structured data objects, such as tables and views.

DELETE—The command used to delete data contained inside a table. Does not delete the table itself.

DISTINCT—The clause used when one wishes to remove duplicate copies of rows in the result set.

DROP—The command used to entirely delete objects from the database.

EXCEPT—Used when the user wants to find the differences between two sets of data. Finds the data from the first table that don't appear in the second table.

EXISTS—Filter condition used to check if a row is present within a table. If the row is present, filter evaluates as true.

FETCH—Method of telling SQL to only return a specified number of records in the result set. E.g., instead of returning every record, only return the first 1,000 records.

FROM—Clause indicating what table or subquery data is drawn from.

GROUP BY—Clause indicating what level of specificity an aggregation should compute across.

GROUPING SETS—Aggregation clause letting the user specify exactly which levels of aggregation are desired without needing to write multiple queries.

HAVING—Similar to the WHERE clause, except operates on aggregated data.

Identity column—A column which generates a unique value every time a new row is inserted.

IIF—Identical to a CASE statement, except simplified syntax, and can only be used for simple comparisons.

IN—A method to compare one value to a list of values for purposes of filtering. Used instead of having multiple **Column** = **value** statements.

Index—A reference table used to enhance the speed of queries.

INSERT—The command used when inserting new data into a table.

INTERSECT—Used when the user wants to find the similarities between two sets of data. Finds the data from the first table that also appears in the second table.

JOIN—Relating two or more tables based on a common attribute.

Key—The identifier that is used to relate two tables to each other.

Literal values—Values that are not found in the table itself. In the query SELECT 'hello', the word "hello" is a literal, because it's not drawn from a table.

MERGE—A method to insert, delete, and update data in a table in a single step, as opposed to multiple steps.

NULL—A missing or unknown value.

OFFSET—Informs SQL how many of the initial rows to skip when displaying results.

ORDER BY—Causes the results of a query to be sorted by the specified column.

OUTER APPLY—A subquery which is invoked like a join, but with the benefit of being able to sort and fetch specific rows rather than just all matching rows.

OUTPUT—Displays the rows from a delete or update query which were altered.

PARTITION BY—Determines the "window" by which window functions are applied.

Pivoting—A method of reorganizing data by moving values within rows to their own columns.

Query—A command sent to the database.

ROLLBACK—The statement used to indicate that the changes made during a transaction should be reverted.

ROLLUP—Clause which calculates the aggregate values according to the specified group, and then successively gets more general by removing the last item from the group, and then aggregating. Process repeats until the aggregate operates across entire data set.

ROWS BETWEEN—Clause indicating how many rows forward or backwards in a partition a window function should operate on.

SELECT—Statement which asks the database to retrieve data.

SOME—The clause used to check how a value compares against some values in another column. E.g., is the value for **PurchasePrice** greater than at least *some* of the values in a different column? Will return true if it is greater than at least one of them.

SQL Server—Microsoft's implementation of the relational database management system.

SQL Server Management Studio (SSMS)—Software program used to administer different parts of SQL Server. Often contains buttons and menu items to complete tasks that are accomplished via queries.

Subquery—A query which is run as part of another query. Typically, must be calculated first in order for main query to return data.

Table—A database object which contains data in the form of columns and rows.

Temporary table—A table which exists only for the duration of the query.

TOP—An alternative to FETCH which tells SQL how many rows to return in the result set.

Transaction—A "unit of work" where one or more changes to the database are held in suspension until either committed or reverted.

TRUNCATE—Command used to completely wipe a table of all data. The table is not deleted.

UNION—Used when two or more tables must be displayed in the same result set, or treated as though all the data is contained within one table.

Unpivoting data—A method of reorganizing data by moving multiple columns into multiple rows within a single column.

UPDATE—Command used to update the existing data in a table.

USE—Informs SQL which database to use when looking for tables.

View—Query that acts like a table. Views can be treated like tables and used in much the same way, except a view doesn't actually store any information.

WHERE—Clause used to filter results based on some condition.

Wildcards—Used when searching for inexact matches. Wildcard can take the place of any character(s).

Window functions—A function, such as an aggregate or ordinal function, that is applied only to a specific set of rows such as rows within a certain proximity, or over a partition.

WITH TIES—When used with TOP and ORDER BY, tells SQL to pull the top rows, plus any additional rows that would be tied for last place, per the sorting method.

www.ingramcontent.com/pod-product-compliance
Lightning Source LLC
Chambersburg PA
CBHW060549060326
40690CB00017B/3652